Insister

Insister
of Jacques Derrida

By Hélène Cixous

Original Drawings by Ernest Pignon-Ernest

Translated by Peggy Kamuf

Stanford University Press
Stanford, California
2007

Stanford University Press
Stanford, California

© Editions Galileé, 2006.
English translation © Peggy Kamuf, 2007
Originally published in France in 2006 by Editions Galilée,
9 rue Linné, 75007 Paris

First published in the UK by Edinburgh University Press Ltd

A CIP record for this book is available from the Library of Congress

ISBN 978-0-8047-5907-6 (cloth)
ISBN 978-0-8047-5908-3 (pbk.)

Typeset in Bembo by
Servis Filmsetting Ltd, Manchester, and
printed and bound in Great Britain

Contents

'I have often declared my admiration for Hélène Cixous, for the person and for the work: immense, powerful, so multiple but unique in this century.'

Jacques Derrida

Insister

Insister
of Jacques Derrida

'It's a vision: you and I are two mice in sports clothes, two lilliputian beings full of life. And we're playing with a ball, football. My mouse is stage right. Yours is a hefty little male and you're getting ready to shoot stage left. My little girl mouse is the goal keeper. She goes back and forth in front of the goal. She's guarding, but at the same time she's very frightened of the shot; she lets go sharp little yelps of apprehension. You are looking at her energetically. Notice: the dreaming woman is on your side. You crouch like a cat ready to shoot. The girl mouse screams at the same time as she cannot stop laughing, since after all it's a game. You're going to score, that's for sure. A force emanates from you. Your little muscled and centered body. The other agitated one who is running everywhere. All at once you burst out laughing: the spectacle of the adversary who is really frightened makes you laugh but benevolently.

'The title of this dream is: Scoring [Marquer]. It comes to sign this text.'

Dream, April 2005.

I

Insister. How to translate that?

– The chase of truth, that's our eternal conversation.

– The chance of the chase. The chase of the chance

– I run after truth, I chase it. Chasing it I chase it away, you say

– Sussing that chasing it you chase it away, I say

– I put in question all assayings, beginning with sayings and other meanings-to-say, and before beginning, beginning with words

– The chase after happiness, that's Stendhal's chase and mine as well.

– The question of truth obsesses me

– You obsess it. One never knows who obsesses whom, who besieges, retains, captures whom, will have begun what

– The question of veracity, even more so; no one can prove anything about lying. Hence my relation to literature.

– Which relation?

– Chance literature. No one will ever catch it lying or truth-telling *in flagrante delicto*. Literature, neither lie nor veracity: no one will ever prove that I am lying

– That's why you have always stayed in closest proximity to literature

– In closest approximity, in the neighborhood. No one will ever prove that I am inside or outside. It so happens that sometimes I happen to find myself there, lost naturally. A naturally lost child.

– But you don't stay there. Literature is your temptation. Between literature and you

– There's naught, but a step. I give three long lectures at the Bibliothèque Nationale Française. I talk about de Man, it's very ambiguous what I'm doing; I talk about Rousseau, the purloined ribbon, perjury, forgiveness. And if I had the time and the space I would consecrate a chapter, two chapters, to what Marion might have thought, two chapters, three chapters giving this thought *entirely free rein*, you insist, letting it unfold in the most fantastic way; if I wrote the way I would like to write, between the coldly analytic passages there would be some utterly fantastical outbreaks, Marion's point of view,

– I see it already

– But I don't do it.

You know my taste for literary writing. I love something *in* literature, without loving it in general and for itself. I confided all of this to *Passions*. Not that

I love literature in general, not that I prefer it to anything else, especially not to philosophy. I can do
without literature easily enough. Yes it's true. Yes it's
true, without loving it in general and for itself, I love
in literature. If I love something in it, it would be *in
the place of the secret*. In the place of an absolute secret.
There would be the passion. If I had the time and
the space, I would consecrate fantastical chapters to
the secret, giving *entirely free rein* to Marion, to what
I might have thought that she might have thought, to
what she might have thought that I might have
thought

– If you wrote as you would like to write, you
'would consecrate.'

– But I don't do it.

I think about the secret. I think about nothing else.
What causes me to suffer: on the one hand I love and
need the secret. On the other the secret attracts indis-
cretion and vulgarity.

I hold on to the secret. I hold in secret. I am held in
secret. I hold to the help, the force of the secret.

– All of your philosophical publications *in the place of
the secret*

– An autobiography in absolute secret. Absolutely
private. All the more so for being public.

– No one will ever be able to prove that you are
lying

You never lie

— You believe that? Or you believe that you believe?

— I believe.

— If only I could believe you.

— No one will ever be able to prove that I don't believe

Myself, I don't believe that I believe; I am certain.

— Don't say 'I am certain.'

— Let's come back to literature. The one that interests us. The one that writes to the undecidable.

— You write to the undecidable

— The undecidable reads me.

— How do you write the undecidable?

— With a capital: the Undecidable.

— Writing that is 'literary,' in other words, undecidabilized has a status of improbability

— It hides itself. It's India. It's China. I adore it. I adore the fact that it hides itself. The chase for 'literary' writing is my chase after happiness. It runs away from me, it's always there for me to chase. Run away! I chase you off. It makes an escape. It makes my landscape

— Happiness, that is to say?

— According to me yes, to read, that is, to see to read as you would say, to write so as to see to read, that is, to see to live, without knowing, to pursue, tirelessly, relentlessly, the being in flight, the letters in flight of beings in flight,

and inversely not to chase, to let come, to let fall rise
the wind the tempest, be found, the time, the weather,
the verb be found listen see, arise perhaps, the unex-
pected adorable sentence, always at the moment at
which we think all is lost, deserted, mute, void
    then – at this then –
    – and always in my absence to myself, –
there may come a sentence, two words, the beating
of a thought.
    I note, you note the idiom: there may come a sen-
tence, that is, '*il* peut arriver *elle, il* se trouve.' I thought
it was *il*, but surprise it's *elle*. In French.
    – 'Happiness, that is to say'
    – That is or that is to say?
    – How do you think I wrote it? Happiness?

★

The sensation when, as we're speaking, you always
speak to me in writing, you speak to me two times at
once, when to hear you I have only the time to stand
quickly to the side, the two sides, mine, yours, so as to
hurry toward the two senses, which I move up or
move back enough to trip on the edge of two unequal
paving stones, the sensation of having an ear that limps
a little and at the same time is offered, alerted, and at
the same time, at the impulse of words the sensation
of being seized by a renewed felicity, all doubt on the

subject of the reality of literary writing finding itself canceled by the enchantment of your delicate idiom – I say

Each time I stumble on the unequal, unequalizable trace, on one of your steps [*pas*], once again joy surges out of uncertainty. Or else: once again uncertainty surges, a joy. It's this inaudible, invisible, infinitesimal disjunction guarding the construction of your sentences in French, this disqualification of certainty that, marvelous paradox, sweeps away all my doubts. And the condition of this enchantment is that there be a certain disordering of the two inside the chant.

★

We met each other in French, as has been said and recounted more than once. Sometimes it makes me tremble. Each determination, overdetermination makes me tremble. In French turned toward English. That must be said. A certain French, ours, a certain English, Joyce's.

— In a French that is accelerated, pushed to the limits, paroxysmized, overexcited, unloosed, frenzied, caressed, delivered, incanted, charmed, attuned, granted, not given, untamable, in a French to another power, stolen, flying, launched toward the to-come, as you would say (to the to-coming) in two words, *à venir*, not to the future, *avenir*, that comes upon us already, but to that to-come that is suspended by the uncertain from its own disjunction

So we met each other in order to think in language, to speak language; between us it has always been a question of writing, of living in language, of hearing ourselves write, so as to write. We speak to one another so as to hear ourselves read, to know how to read, to write ourselves speaking, to give ourselves the writing that is in speech, sometimes so as to take words from each other's mouth.

When it comes to his sentences, I am insatiable, I'm mad about them, since 1963, since 'La parole soufflée,' I'm blown away by them, lifted off my feet and reassured by them. His folisophy, his philslipophy, his silkwormery authorize my risking-writing to scare itself with saying more than enough, with not saying more than enough, more than I know.

Right away we reassured each other: no one enters here except through anxiety, in anxiety. We recognized one another in anxiety and in foreignness. Thought thinks only by becoming foreign to itself, by losing consciousness. Right away we worried each other.

So I have been reading you since I cannot stop myself, stop myself from writing as from breathing. Saying that I *resuck-citate* your saying in period 5 'I posthume as I breathe,'[1] your cruel and fabulous saying. I read you day by day since I have been writhing in my own furrows, as if you were natural to me, fated.

I open at random and at will any text at any page, certain as I am to find what for. What what for? Always at least two whats. Something is going to happen. I read you out of need, desire, vital curiosity, together, for some glorious event of writing (for example the *glorious appeasement*). In order *to breathe*. When I read you, I breathe.

A little of the anxiety that grips my throat, holds me by the throat, loosens. A little of the anxiety that has to do with the throat, the *gorge*, the word *gorge*, which I get from my father Georges, the georgic word, and you did not fail to note the g,[2] the geological layer of the *g* in my text, so as to lodge it [*le loger*] in the shelter of yours, give *g* lodging [*lui* g], and all its gems coursing through the veins of languages.[3]

As for you, what holds you by the throat is the *gl*. Barely had I opened 'Circumfession,' I remember, I had 'begun' with the first period, first masterpiece of the fifty-nine chants that will forever more rival one another for the title of masterpiece of masterpieces, and, carried away by a long fervor, I found myself in a street in Algiers in my your childhood, where I lived literally each shimmering second of this mystical scene, from word to word of the incantation, experience for which your voice was the shaman, and my thought,

14

entirely tinted with old and familiar images, cradled in your sentence, beneath the arcade of its stairway, inhaled the perfume that, to the one who returns home after a long voyage, instantly gives back the unique keys to the place that guards memory. From this period there arises an aroma that mixes hot dust blood ether orange blossoms urine, a whole spice shop that forces a cry of recognition. It was Algiers. And (yet) it was you. A mutual and very powerful resurrection. (I say 'Algiers.' But I hasten to add that this is a name for countless interior and exterior mysteries, like the name of Venice or the name of God.) This period is a blast furnace, I say. God knows what aspirations, reminiscences, beliefs, moods, philosophical professions are being alloyed there.

Today I know this period almost by heart, not that I wish ever to master it, not that I seek to understand it, but as if by force of reading it, that is, of being carried beyond myself by its current, it had joined up in me, along paths reserved exclusively for the psalmody of poems, with the minimal religious cavity where prayers and recitations are kept apart: long utterances that accumulate a surplus sacred force with each repetition.

'Le vocable cru,' 'The crude word,' I murmured, and I took a breath so as to let flow a sentence that is barely a sentence, up to 'ce que j'appelai: le glorieux apaisement,' 'what I called: the glorious appeasement'

And it is as if I had said 'Derrida' otherwise, the thousand and one names or words of this name. It is as if in order to say Derrida I had to pass by way of the spelling of an immense antonomasis of blood.

For each segment, thus dissociated, and absolutely indissociable of this sentence, each breath and phrase of this phrase, still untamed and so wise, each instant can only be you, only by you, only issued from the superpowerful machine that makes you proffer and whose secret even you do not know.

(One day it will be necessary to draw the portrait of the signature, the stamp, not the style, there is no style, the mark, like a genetic code in language. You, for example, unlike Blanchot, for example, who anteposes in order to register his mark, you rush ahead doubling your speed; you are always already further on; you don't leave anyone the time to have-read-you; you put an advance spin on each syntagma, without counting the commas you sow to shake off and delay the pursuers. Art of semantation.)

This phrase, period, that I thought to take, overtake by speeding up, whereas, by turns rapid and bent over its mythological wheel, not Proust's wheel but yours, the one that rolls and racks, it had taken me, this phrase that while I abandon myself to reading (is that the

16

word?), changing voice by turns clear juvenile strangled by the fear of relief, gives me back lost life, I
remember that it deposited me completely dizzy, after
the two dots of a colon posted like the threshold of an
adieu or of a 'get off,' before the words: the glorious
appeasement.

    . . . but only one sentence, scarcely a sentence, the plural
    word of a desire toward which all the others since always
    seemed, confluence itself, to hurry, an order suspended
    on three words, *find the vein*, what a nurse might
    murmur, syringe in hand, needle upward, before *taking
    blood*, when for example in my childhood, and I remember that laboratory in a street of Algiers, the fear and
    vagueness of a glorious appeasement both took hold of
    me, took me blind in their arms at the precise moment
    at which by the point of the syringe there was established
    an invisible passage, always invisible, for the continuous
    flowing of blood, absolute, absolved in the sense that
    nothing seemed to come between the source and the
    mouth, the quite complicated apparatus of the syringe
    being introduced in that place only to allow the passage
    and to disappear as instrument, but continuous in that
    other sense that, without the now brutal intervention of
    the other who, deciding to interrupt the flow once the
    syringe, still upright, was withdrawn from the body,
    quickly folded my arm upward and pressed the swab

inside the elbow, the blood could still have flooded, not indefinitely but continuously to the point of exhausting me, thus aspirating toward it what I called: the glorious appeasement.[4]

There would be enough to write a book on this sentence-scene, on the scenes in the sentences, on the concentricities around the syringe axis, on the apparatus, the architecture of the event whose figure is comparable to Dante's Inferno, and in its whirlwind of time in ascending descension, ascendantesquely, on the representation, phantasm mixed with reality of this confrontation of bodies between the one who draws the blood and the one who lets it be drawn between the nurse-critic-reader-analyst-laboratory assistant and the exhaustible-inexhaustible child, between the two who fight over the vein in the obscurity of a struggle that does not say its name, father and son (but father and son exchange places), Jacob with the angel, on the secret, on the *agons* and agonies, on the submission, resistance, decision, floods, taken seriously, simulated, performed, outsmarted, on the overabundant resources of Paradox, the river along whose shore begins Hades, on the strange forces that take the child into their arms to vanquish him and glorify him, the blind child, but solely on the two dots of the colon, those of the: *glorious appeasement*, a staggering, superb, chilling expression, that sends into silence the specter of a peace whose name must not be spoken.

With these words I got off the sentence.

– This is not the first time I have heard this *gl* sounded. 'The glorious appeasement' this insistence at the end of a sentence.

– Orgasm, outpouring, an expression invented at the moment. It seemed to me to resemble what I wanted to say, with the *gl*, with the light, you say

The first period came both spontaneously, as if from the source, and then like something come from far away.

– Like the source and the cutting off of the source

– Afterwards it settled.

Afterwards he rewrites a lot but not tampering with the flow, little things, commas, a rhythm.

The event becomes more and more thought out, incited, calculated, receives laws, gets put in place, recognizes itself as event whose advent has happened to literature, not just to the little boy from Algiers.

★

Often we tell each other these adventings of texts. Storms happen to us

Sometimes I want to flee the squall that I want to pinpoint. But I am already soaked.

We see clearly the other's blindness. But we are careful not to say: you don't see what you don't see?

★

I am reading you. From-the-first-day you speak (to me) of dying

Book after text speech lecture. Since 1963. Already in 1955. I listen to you. I believe you at your word, I believe your word, your heart, and I don't believe you.

Resistance? Rather: obedience. Obedience to life. Obedience of life to your life. Obedience to your desire not to die.

– But who is talking about living? (The tone? How to translate it? It's you, it's he who is talking about living.) Living, I don't think about it. I live.

Living? you say. And from the first days he asks me if I believe it is going to last. But who can speak, speak well, of living? As if one could speak, speak well, of living, etc. I want to say to him: Live. But if I say: live, I deliver division. And he wants the first sweetness to *last*.

I believe you and I don't believe you. Simultaneously. You, I believe you, me I don't believe you. I believe betwixt. You too in a certain way. You betwixt more than I believe. You believe and count on me, that I believe adamantly, *dur comme fer*. I write *faire* otherwise.

We fight over words, the meanings and the directions of the pointers, like the hands of the clock or the needle of a syringe.

I read you. How not to believe you? When I read you I am with you, it's you who aren't with you.

I fight you over yourself.

You try to join up with H.C. for life against the unnamable. I pretend to be H.C.

★

I am reading you. It's Monday, 18 April 2005. That's it, this Monday is future, it is past. I am reading you at present and there is no present. Everything is present and there is no present. It's enough to make you crazy, especially in French. As long as I read there is only some present a certain present, which you would call spectral perhaps. I read: you are.

I think in French, I prefer to. Here, in French, the present always has two values, one in actuality, one in eternity. (Contrary to English where one marks the difference between actuality and the gnomic present, but I prefer not to think of English, *je file à l'anglaise*, I slip away.)

– Here, that's where?

– It's a segmented construction, says my daughter.

– Here that's where, I say to myself.

You sorted it out, the present. It's like your 'at this very moment,' and all these values of time, of the time, in French that you gave yourself the trouble, and the bitter pleasure, of deconstructing.

– At this very moment I write you, I read you. From my point of view. I write this from my point of view. No one will be able to dispute me. The situation of the utterance can only be subjective.

You can always not believe me. And perhaps you cannot neither believe me nor not believe me.

At this very moment here the superimpossible takes place. It takes place where.

★

– But who is talking of the present? 'Now' is also the instants contained up until now.

– I write to maintain the now [*maintenant*], in my hand [*main*], and in good order

– The sentence that I am writing at this moment (at *x* instant) is not the one that you read at this moment (at *y* instant). Today is a past. Tomorrow, there will be another past.

– What I write is *xy*. I read you is in the eternal present.

You talk all the time about no-time
— One day, when I will have the time . . ., you say.

★

Interruption with my brother

— You remember when we used to spin like tops?
I am sitting next to my brother, there is no time.
— We tried to make ourselves dizzy, to catch vertigo, says my brother.
As if one could catch what runs after us, like Jacques Derrida running after language that ran after him while trying to circumvent it.
— We spun around on ourselves until we got dizzy.
— We did it together?
— Side by side in the dining room
— Until everything started turning, the room turned around us, the world took off in another direction
— We threw ourselves against the wall while waiting for it or for us to stop turning all by ourselves
— We ran to grab on to Mama's legs, we were afraid that the dizziness would make us fall
— We create an unnatural sensation in our own organism says my brother

– We did it the two of us. We were afraid to go mad all alone. We made the world turn round but then it was we who were turned out

★

Force of hearing

I read you by ear, yes, I read you by hearing.[5]

– My ear is geared to read you, the hearing that never sleeps, from the dawn of the book, right away with the title, right away with the subtitle, I become multiple, I run through three books at once, enough to make anyone stagger, I read you from the golden edge of time

you remember how one used to say in Algeria: Look! Look! to mean listen, listen, *list, list, o list, pay attention*, look with your ears, pay with the ear

oh yes, it's as if ceaselessly, from sentence to sentence, you were saying to me: look! And yes, I 'look,' all ears, and I admire, I become a birddog so as not to lose the trail. I use every aid to aid my hearing. As soon as reading, delirious, I write. I see it: your text wants to read them all that only writing, what you call writing, sows and scatters. All at the same time read, read, read, read and never yet never – the more I read you the more I see to read, reading to infinity

See reading watch out reading madreading morereading overreading underreading doubtfulreading doublereading oblivireading

I avail myself of reading's veil. I read you, in short.

I read you as one must read as soon as there is reading to be done, some to-be-read. As soon as there is some to-be-read and not some read-it-all, as you alone today write, you the only one to write these days of the twentieth and twenty-first centuries, like no one else, like some rare ones, some poor *happy few*, and then reading grows, being raised up it rises, its impact

Pax!

You tell me: you exaggerate. You tell me: continue

You insist that I read you. I insist on reading you. I consist in reading you. I read you so as to consist, to hold myself up. To hold myself back, to hold you back on my side by heart.

★

I read with you your work, with your superyou inside and beyond your work, me with my work. I don't know who reads you when I read you whom I'm reading.

You say to me 'Hallelouïya.' We're having fun. *Allez où il y a*. Always we're making fun of the present, the pleasantry of the present, the passingness of the present

It is not a joke

On the contrary: torment, at the source, of the source.

– Responsibility: to accept the division of truth, the diverity of verity

– To accept, humbly, with the anguish that is a joy, that to think – in other words to live living – is not what we think. You complicate life.

Without cruelty, with humble gratitude toward those who will have lent him an ear – and without alibi.[6]

★

You say to me: go read, there, *allez lis, là*. Go and read. I go. And read. Every sentence you pronounce divides into pointers by the time I receive it. Juggler, I say.

Often distressed (*navré*, the word *navré*) you say to me: who is going to read this? (You ask yourself/you ask me, for yourself, for me as well.)

I say to you: *tu me mets la puce à l'oreille*, 'you put the flea in my ear,' but it means, you give me a hint. In the past and up until La Fontaine the expression meant to have an amorous desire, but that is the past; then the expression came to mean to puzzle to arouse suspicion. In the electronic era, the *puce* is the memory chip that has a power you dream of.

I translate the flea you put in my ear into *question*. Barely have I lent an ear to your text before I feel myself summoned, given notice to wonder, questioned,

26

dislodged from any response that I might think I was able to lodge, pushed further, further and further. You never give up 'problematizating,' putting in question the question itself, the drawing and quartering of every utterance.

As for you, you never say yes. You say yes, yes, *oui, oui,* at least, you doubtfulize everything that presents itself to thought, you split in two so as, you say, to be *consequent.* And you make the word consequent resonate from out of its original Latin – I have to follow you in Latin, in Greek, in German, in secret. You are always in a state of consequence, of sequence, you follow yourself therefore you precede yourself, you pay attention to what follows, to what results, to what is going to follow, later:

> My question will be, rather and later [I underscore]: Is there, for thought, for psychoanalytic thought to come, another beyond, if I can say that, a beyond that would stand beyond these possibles that are still both the pleasure and reality principles and the death or sovereign mastery drives, which seem to be at work wherever cruelty is on the horizon? . . .
>
> I will try, later [I underscore], to argue my salvation with reasons. But before I begin, assuming that I ever begin, I must, when all is said and done and in view of the business of the impossible that I just suspended . . .[7]

The scene of reading is a scene of analytical, critical Passions – but active, inventive ones – and it is edged round by an almost transparent border of spiritual difference that prevents me from ever touching otherwise than indirectly your being, from ever stumbling and falling into the illusion of identification. Between two intimacies a tear that unseparates with a vapor. I read you with a naked ear, with a misty eye. I follow/I am the edge of your French. All the characters play all the roles, each one in its turn (one must try to imagine the complication you expect from each of them, you with your text before you, behind you, on your shoulders) and more or less at the same time. Each one takes part in the game, generalized partaking, taking apart and parting the take. The participants must participate/think, be divided into spectator and actor, be invented as spectactor and lactor.

All yes All hearing [*Tout oui Tout ouïe*], that is what we are, I am twice hearing, hearing for you and hearing of you, from the first day, before any face, before the very first, before, before, from the instant before the very first where without knowing or willing, on your part or on mine, without part therefore, your *parole* seized hold of my hearing without my ever saying no or yes to an address, your speech, that is to say, your writing, the speech of your writing, of your *to write*, in the infinitive

★

I said 'from the first day', we don't know which day exactly will have been the first, for there is also the original and the one before, there is the prophetic, the secret first day the sacred first day the godforsaken first day; each time unique as you would say but who knows who will have said it first, you say, coming from before the farthest we agree to hesitate, we divide the first time we devise conversation on it, we estimate it, we titrate it as well, *the title*, again one of those words, so little, a ti(t)tle, and you draw from it a whole titlizing, in *Le Titrier*, the title in which is the title, the title in which there is some title, the titling, the titler.[8]

★

How you love the power of little words or the condensation, thunderbolt, cunning in these little beings. You dream of a suitcase word, as one says, a portmanteau word, a word for words a miniaturized secret drawer or mirror, light as a feather, quick and clairvoyant as an eagle, little as a *oui*, a *qui*, a *lis*, a *vi*, no bigger than a *J* capable of the whole world a sea/shell for a philosophical kernel, a teetering, needling word, folding and unfolding, a nanoword. A concise key. A comesee.

Alljoyce in two words. And what words! You're the one who found them in the midst of twelve thousand.

I had lent you the index, the *keys*, the chests of words, the dictionaries. Unfortunately I forgot to ask you how you pinpointed '*He war*' so as to lodge there the universe, all of mythology, religions, history, philology, apocalypses.

There are two hypotheses: either, as was known to happen, the two words leapt out at you, or else you were looking to pick a quarrel, you went straight to *war* in the index and you found it waiting for you since forever. In my opinion the two possibilities made just one leap.

★

We take each other at our words, we give each other this word and that word, and that word, you know it (*hernie, géhenne, volubilis, mansuétude, perroquet, jacquot-petrus*, individuals, families, semantemes, signifiers' shards, *tessons, tes sons* in French and *sons* in English) we are like those animals busy sniffing and unearthing dictionaries, we lift out expressions, that one do you hear it? 'Il faut s'attendre,' 'il était temps,' we slip by each other, we wait for each other at the police checkpoint, at the borders, do you hear that? *Oui je m'y attendais* (Yes I was expecting it, I was waiting for myself there). *Je t'y attendais* (I was expecting you, I was waiting for you there). *Je m'attends à ce que tu t'attendes à ce que je t'entende. Il faut s'attendre*: one has to expect/wait for oneself/another. You overturn expectations, you surprise, it is your way of according grace.

Did not everything between us begin 'for good' with *a word*?

What she had written to me, before our encounter, was not a true letter, no doubt, but a postcard, a very hasty word, from afar, from the provinces (from somewhere near Arcachon or Bordeaux, near Montaigne, I believe, where, if I am not mistaken, she used to teach some thirty-five years ago).[9]

With these words the quarrel starts up again between us, it animates us, what is a true letter? A P.C.? A word? Starting from which date, weight, form does one become the other? Which word? A word in how many words? Between us the whole game has always turned, and been decided destinally, on words, on their promise, on their undecidability, hesitationally. Asifinquotationally. Long words, I say, give time and space to reflect. But one must go quickly all the same. As for him, he says that life is short. Mme de Sévigné also says this, but I don't tell him that. He alone says these words with that tone.

More than once we say the same words or we advance on the impulse of like expressions, but we do not live them in the same tone.

Most of the time he is more 'modalizing' than I in the mode of attenuation, reticence. Modalization in the language which responds to his never mollified sense of responsibility, to that ethical mistrust with regard to authority, which makes him prudent. Let's take a few of the sentences that paint him painting the event of the encounter between the two of us:

I-met-her-some-thirty-five-years-ago-maybe.

And although I have probably never understood anything about it, although I have not understood her yet, we have probably never been apart. It is as if we had almost never been apart.

Yes, I believe, I-met-her-some-thirty-five-years-ago-maybe.[10]

1) I met her – maybe –
2) And although
3) It is as if
4) Yes, I believe

That's him all right, and it's not me at all I say. He underlines *as if* and *almost*. I would also underline *perhaps*, *probably*, *no doubt*, *I believe*. I read him:

As if and *almost*, it's as if and as if, a tautology that is not one. All the force is in the *almost* that bears on the *never been apart.* Almost crosses out and confirms the utterance. So, then, what?

Here is a sentence that in its redoubled hypothetical prudence says something undecidable. Reader, think twice about it, because the subject of the utterance says one thing that is another thing. Maybe.

Almost never, neither never nor its opposite.

But is it possible almost never to be apart? Is it possible never to be apart without ever being apart? *Sans jamais se quitter? Et toi, qui t'es?* And you, who're you? No doubt the one who puts in question doubt and the no doubt.

★

I follow/I am the edge of your text. It is jagged, rocky, foamy with waves, salty, it makes one think of the coast of our country, next I will tell you what I found.

– You say that to please me.

But it is your refound text that pleases you. I am merely giving it back to you in a portrayal. I am reading your cards.

How I read (you) your text on the one hand as a musical score on the other hand as in a dream, as in a painting, from the middle, from one side or the other, like a seagull dives into the ocean, as when I stop for a long time on the threshold of Rembrandt's *Bœuf écorché*, to the comma, attentive to the comma, as well as to the hyphen, to their sudden withdrawal, to their spectral insistence

As if I were listening to the murmured circumfession that each one of your texts hides itself as, attempting itself, fleeing, praying, conjuring itself. It is your voice that I read at the portal of your text. No one has ever read a text so mysteriously, secretly inexplicably auto-biographical, from start to finish, as your philosophy. Even your most professionally philosophical, most universally political texts arise out of your soul wrenchings.

★

– That is certainly you. That is certainly well concealed. Say I.

– You know, you say.

You don't say: I know. An I know would be Absolute Knowledge, the attribute of Sovereignty. You say: 'You know.'

– Me, I know?

– You know.

– If you say so, then that's because it's true. I believe everything you say or write. I have taken your side.

– You know, you say

– So be it, I say.

– And I, you say, I don't know. I didn't know, you say in *Veils*. One doesn't know. How to know what?

No one can meet another except beyond knowing.

Absolutely

I have always read you two times at once and on faith at least two times and at two times.

– Yourself, I read you, you, thinking it, suffering, laughing, you your own book to write. As if you were a living looming book. Altogether speech, sentences, signs (body, soul, destiny)

– Always facing before you or beside as before a Bible but undecipherable

This Living Book is accompanied doubled by your books

– Antonomasis: a man–who–writes. A species. Who thinks to write. Who asks himself: what is writing? What is philosophy? Who makes of *thinking* a brand new word. A man by the side of the other, on the other cat or woman by the rib.

Likewise reading books, I read the subject and the one saying (Stendhal). Rare conjunction.

– Complicated, in movement, in the process of, self-styled 'self-analyst,' auscultating yourself, feeling out yourself and in the other.

Uninterrupted conversation, ours, equivocal polyvocal you, the text (the work), the opus, the corpus,

– 'Seeing' also the next book coming, before seeing – before you see, before I see, listening to the murmur of yourself at the edge of yourself

With the result that reading your books, alive read-ingness, reading me to you, I have always instantly responded to you, on the telephone.

★

How will I know that I am reading you?

By the feeling of being, by your reading, read. Read naked. No one can read you, read you well (with a reading 'worthy of the name' – that's what you would say, you who believe there is something like worthiness, dignity, you who wants it), without exposing herself/himself, without being exposed to a baring of the soul, double nakedness of the one read and the one reading.

There are conditions on this reading/writing at risk, double risk, that of being read and that of being not read. There must be a nakedness. There must be a modesty. There must be a non-indecent non-decency.

'Every other is altogether other,' as you will have justly – just man that you are – insisted, on the irre-ducible, the insurmountable, and the tragic, but desir-able, difference. And yet as altogether other every other is my fellow kind, there is beyond the just and what you say about it particularly, 'I know not what inexplicable and fatal force'[11] that makes you universal.

I read myself to you, reading you in your altogeth-erotherness I am read. Thereupon you read me in my altogetherotherness, unknown to myself

– You are always closest to the source, he says. Me, between the source and me, there are mountains of pipes and tubes, a real racket. If one listens hard one hears the source all the same.

– One day we'll do a seminar on *la source et le tuyau*, the source and the pipe. What is a pipe, a *tuyau*? Who gives a pipe/*tuyau*? In Gothic it was a horn.

Once more, always, a muted horn, a fold, a secret, a confiding, the call launched too late, so that it would be too late, pure call, by the last of the 'Jews,' by the last of the 'Christians.'

★

He reads everything I write. Then he forgets and remembers. Both at once. Then he rereads. At some moment.

– I just reread *Beethoven Forever* (or *Manhattan*, or *Portrait of the Sun*) he says to me.

– Why?

– I was in my mezzanine, I took the book off the shelf. That's why.

For the secret. For literature.

He asks himself: what is reality?

Italics thus keep the reality of what is said to have taken place in reality in suspense, in literature. The italics give us to think, even bring into play, the very body of the question: What is reality? What is an event? What is a past event? And what does 'past' or 'come to pass' mean, etc.? So many uncertainties or aporias for whoever claims to bring order within a library, between the library and its outside, the book and the non-book, literature's and its others, the archivable and the non-archivable.

Therein is found literature secret, the infinite power to keep undecidable and thus forever sealed the secret of what it/she says, it, literature, or she, Cixous, or even of what it/she avows and that remains secret, even as in broad daylight it/she avows, unveils or claims to unveil it.[12]

Sometimes he addresses the secret. He asks my text how it happens what happens in his text unbeknownst to every institution.

He is even on the brink of asking me a realist question. I see him sketch a 'what happened?' Is he going to rend us with the beating of a drunken wing?[13] And then, no, the philosopher stops him at the edge. At the invisible edge of the fictional.

Sometimes he addresses this Library that I am, asking with an admirable hesitation if he wasn't perhaps in the process of discovering for the first time something new to write that if he reread a certain text by H.C. would (re)appear to him already written for the first time, as he will have confided in several pages of *Geneses* (pp. 66–64), with a purity that is unique (I am weighing my words), in the history of literature

He will have done here the most beautiful act, the most beautiful act of grace that I know. Revelation without guilt, in a parenthesis, of a kinship untouched by legacy between two altogether other writings that will never have ceased finding themselves/each other.

He says it a thousand times better than I can. In truth I must assist and insist that the gift – the giving the givingly, not the donation – will have been accorded at a single blow, to the one as to the other to each of the other, no one will ever know how. Furthermore how could he not be 'the first' to find 'the thing' that he finds, and the thing that, if it is found, I might have found another time, in another history, another story, 'in advance' otherwise and very often without my having appropriated 'the thing' and even without having 'kept' it?

★

– I'm rereading *The First Name of God*. Everything is in there.

He announces this to me on the telephone, in March 1998. *The First Name of God*? What is he telling me here? Except for the First Name, I don't have the least idea about *The First Name of God*, I don't want to hear about it. How to tell him that? This is the text that fell on him, that hit us like a blow, almost forty years ago

'Read and don't say anything.' How to tell him that?

Even I don't understand myself, I especially don't want to understand myself, it would be terrible if I saw. I'm entirely given over to my fear, to my flight. Let no one speak to me about it, ever! How to say to him: there are books that I signed and forgot, but because they had to be kept forgotten, there are books that must remain at a distance from my being, there are books that know too much and not enough. This has never happened to him, on the contrary. Everything he has written, from his first schoolboy's notebooks, he can look in the face.

– There is everything. I understand why I received such a warning. I have even discovered the tallith there. My tallith! Do you remember?

– No, no, I swear I have no memory of it. I remember only his tallith.

I will not go see. I did not return.

'Today'

'Everything has changed'   'Nothing has changed'

I write these two sentences on the same line but sepa-
reunifying them with a 'blank,' a voiceless, bottomless,
depthless spacing. Today 10 March 2005, I write the
word today. Today, a word that you give us with
great frequency. I just stumbled on a today, one of
your numerous todays, the one on to which I have just
stumbled, tripped, staggered, and thus begun to think,
is situated page 17 *États d'âme* . . .

> By attempting to take another step, I will be asking
> whether, today, here and now, the word and the concept
> of resistance still remain appropriate. Do they represent
> the most strategic, most economical lever for thinking
> what is going wrong, what is not going well in the world

on the subject and in the vicinity of psychoanalysis, between it and it, if I can say that? What is going wrong? What is not going well? What is suffering and complaining? Who is suffering from what? What is the grievance of psychoanalysis? What registers of mourners has it opened? To be signed by whom?[14]

– but I open *Resistances*, it is there from the first page. It is today a little bit everywhere with you. It's what the weather's like, it's the time of day. How many todays, a herd, an army, the word of cunning and naïvety, the impossible today that's yours, *le vierge, le vivace, le bel* the rebel today.

A signature, a word that you privilege, uproot replant, make pivot, surplus-value, overvalue, from one day to the other text, that you persecute, that expects your perjury, that you make into a perjury, that makes you a perjurer, perjurcuter, that turns you into a ram drives you up a wall, you will never have stopped todaying one has only to read you I say to myself and instantly you today with your eternal mischievousness, you have always been ready for everything, ready and prepared, for absence like presence, absence like the other presence, presence like the other absence, I have only to read you, and you are here. Here and now, it's enough to make you laugh. – Laugh or weep? You say – Laugh, weep, laughweep, we say, it's the same. – Do you hear what you have just written what I have just read?

A word that has not changed at all will never change his way of working a text, of pricking it, spurring it, making it stagger, or to add another recurrent, insisting word, '*marcher*,' walk, work, run, etc., 'making it work, run,' putting a text in motion, turning it on and on time –

the same word, totally changed in my eyes, in my soul, sent, sent away, before me, by the wounded heart of my soul, – of my 2005 thinking so changed since last year and yet the same, this today, a later today, loaded with messages and lurking thoughts. It is here now, you say, this today, you say, which one I say, the one of the year 2000 you say, listen, I am talking to you you say, here now, I read you today I say, the one of the year 2005, the same, and so what do you say? Here, page 45 of *États d'âme* . . . you say, I take perhaps a few steps (you always take a few steps, a few *pas*, don't you?) (perhaps):

I would perhaps have taken a few steps in the direction of the self-analysis that I was evoking a moment ago. My own, perhaps, which does not interest many people, barely myself, for example around the questions that made me choose to speak to you today about the death drive, as I have done too often, but especially about cruel suffering, and that cruelty that is found at the center of a seminar, the last one, that I thought I had to devote elsewhere, and this is not fortuitous, to the death penalty. But well beyond my own, which is not worthy of your attention, it is the direction of the self-analysis of the Estates General of Psychoanalysis that I will take my chances more surely.[15]

And now you worry about the translators, the man or woman translator, how is he is she going to read you, is he is she going to be able to, you worry, with that emotion of tenderness, always on the alert here – you say, you confess, that once again you've made them a present. Thus a poisoned present. You believe –

You are quite embarrassed about it, you are delighted about it

you disculpate yourself of what you accuse yourself of, you know (that) you don't know what you have done yet

psychoanalysis would be, I said at the outset, the only possible approach, and without alibi, to all the virtual translations between the cruelties of a suffering 'for the pleasure of it', of the making-suffer or the letting-suffer in this way, of the making-oneself or letting-oneself suffer, oneself, one another, the ones and the others, and so forth, according to all the grammatical persons and the implicit verbal modes – active, passive, middle voice, transitive, intransitive, and so on. Wrongly, in contradiction with these premises, the conclusion one has just read might then seem to accredit at least one difference between two crimes, between two transgressions of the 'Thou shalt not kill': between, on the one hand, the murder that consists in killing the other, in him- or herself or in oneself, and, on the other hand, what is commonly called suicide, or the crime against oneself . . .

if a forgiveness can be asked, according to good common sense, for the evil inflicted, for the wrong, the crime, the offense of which the other is, by my doing, the victim, can I not also have to be forgiven the evil I am suffering from? 'Forgive me for the hurt I feel, my heart, there where no one wants to hurt me, for hence comes the hurt I do to you without wanting to, without faith or law, *sans foi ni loi* . . .'

Avoir mal, faire mal, vouloir du mal, en vouloir à quelqu'un (to feel hurt, to cause hurt, to wish evil, to begrudge someone): I already imagine the sufferings of the translator who would like to respect each of these three words: *d'avoir à faire mal à quelqu'un* (to have to hurt someone), not to mention *vouloir du mal à quelqu'un* (to wish hurt or evil on someone). An apparently impossible translation. The French language seems to me the only one that deals out such a fate or such a welcome to the unheard-of and absolutely singular configuration of these words, these very large words: *avoir, faire, vouloir,* and *mal.*

– Am I somehow to blame for this impossibility of translation? For the impossibility of translating word for word?

– No, of course not, it's in the language. You inherit it.

– Yes I am, on the contrary; look what I'm doing with this inheritance. I'm betraying its truth.

– Is the alibi still avoidable? Is it not already too late?[16]

You accuse yourself of that which you are innocent –
It is endless, the ring of guilt, you slip it on yourself –
You worry that you have once again written some *pasje* – apparently impossible to translate (to the ear: *pages*; to the eye: *notI* or *stepsI*). And you congratulate yourself. It is what you desire and what you wish for yourself, to be always the last of the last, the very first and the last. Your followers-pursuers, whom you are careful to shake off, are between you and yourself, you in advance and you in *après*-sence

'I already imagine', you say; the 'apparently impossible translation'

– 'Am I somehow to blame for this impossibility of translation?' says one of your ghost voices. Ghost-voice-ghost-writer.

– No of course not says one of your voices

– Yes of course – you say to yourself

You think all the time *à la* translation – (yet another idiomatic French form) with the help of, in the direction of, by force of, you think across yourself, all crossed up with translation, you write with several voices and each one of your ghosts thinks of the other, with the other . . .

You think all the time of defying it, calling to it. Your thinking ventures into the regions of the not yet and the perhaps, zones of trembling approaches, surprises, surceases. Of all those *sur*'s that launch thought beyond its limits.

To go there, into these groundless, bottomless regions, you invent fragile and supple sur-words.

I read you. Chance would have it that I was already of your language, chance of destiny, chance of two destinies which we knew nothing about at the beginning when we arrived each one from his or her side by the same route and the same path from an outer-edge of France to the other edge, called, pushed and called each of us, by his or her desire, a mad irresistible desire, to move toward the heights, toward the north, and the head, toward the capital of the language, dashing straight, each one for himself, for herself toward the lips and the tongue – of French,

each one of us, transported before knowing by the vital need to go gather up as close as possible to the source the flow of the language.

You think *à la* translation I say —

Which does not mean that you write thinking of translation into foreign languages. It is the foreignness, the strangeness of French that strikes you, that you cause to spurt, to spring up again, that you make resonate, the strangeness yours, the one you feel as soon as you rub against this language that you have and that is not yours. It is in the narrow margin of the 'monolingualism of the other' that you find yourself and that I am going to look for you.

Among all other languages, the language that speaks French or that the French speak or that are spoken in French, an exacerbated language, galloping until it's carried away, bit between the teeth, overexcited, overidiomed, capable of every kind of mobility in the world, that of the bird, that of the feline, that of the ant, that of the poem, that of Time, that of the unconscious, you initiated by Gide (J.D.) me at Joyce (James?) that of the Swan, which is to say of the *Cygne*, which is to say of the Sign

up to the drunken beating of the wing, the *coup d'aile ivre*

up to the blow of the books, the *coup des livres*

To read in order to deliver with a beating of the wings, with a drunken blow by her, *d'un coup d'aile, d'un coup d'elle ivre*, the transparent glacier of the flights that have not flown

Un cygne d'autrefois se souvient que c'est lui

Tearing, torn, this lecture, but also delivering, *magnifique mais qui sans espoir se délivre*

Beneath the ice, beneath the ice

I'm alarmed by you I say

Tu ne l'as pas volé, you asked for it. *Pour n'avoir pas chanté la région où vivre*

— Je ne l'ai pas volé you say. How to translate that? 'I asked for it,' yes, but no: 'I didn't steal it,' 'I didn't fly it.'

Library, archive of stolen flights in flight but always ready should the ice be broken to take again to the air

I do not stop reading you, you do not stop speaking to me 'today,' of today.

What am I saying there? How do I say this saying?

I listen to myself. I repeat myself. I hear:

1) First, right away, I say *you*, that is, *tu*.

Where did I si*tu*ate myself? Where if you are I, *si tu es je* — I am you, I follow you —

In the interior forum you speak of in *Rams* —

In the forum of uninterruption.

2) I read you: you read yourself to me. You speak to me. This *tu* speaks to me. You play on the *tu*.[17] You tease me this sentence. Certain times you say to me: *tu parles!* [You're telling me, you must be joking, you bet, but also simply, you speak!] This *tu speaks (to) us*. As you would say that the animal looks at us.

Most often, speaking of him in writing, I say *you*, that is, *tu*. This *you* is not in my control, it is stronger than me. As for him, you say rather 'she' of me. He says Hélène, or Hélène Cixous, or H.C.

When, in my seminar, I share him with my friends or listeners, it's 'Derrida' that I offer to a reading, that I extend. It's because he is, since forever, this *tu* in me that speaks, who speaks of who speaks of living, my complication, my accomplice, my interior force stronger than me. But everyone knows that there is more than one *tu*, he himself made the innumerable and complex inventory in *Geneses* . . .

To whom is she speaking, with these months and me's, you [*tu*] and you [*vous*] so as to recount my death, yours, your death, and your faces; your death can be hers, that of the me who is speaking and who speaks to herself, the one spoken of from the other place of the dream or the death of the you [*tu*] who, further on, in the same paragraph will be dissected, we shall see, with all the resources of its untranslatable homonymy, that is, of these irreducible French homonymies, whose language all dreams recall (*tu* meaning *toi, t, u, tu*, that which is struck dumb with the silence of the verb *taire* and *se taire* [to hush, hush up], *le tu* [the you, the silenced] of the secret, *le tu* as the genius of the secret: genius *qui est tu* [who is you, who is silenced], etc. Just as months of tears have gone by, like a period of time and the

50

multiplicity of I's or me's who are others, four weeks and just so many *egos*, so there is the *tu* who is you and knows to fall silent or impose silence concerning itself).[18]

There is one for him, one for you, one for the National Library.

Yet this *tu* is indeed him, the one who speaks to me in the tube of the so-very-interior ear that right away I say *tu* to him, I echo internally – Io! – it is the young and green and perpetual *tu*, which I clearly hear, it's true, rise up from among the *tu*'s that have fallen silent or been killed, *tus* or *tués*, or don't know who you are who silences, *qui tu es qui tait*.

Yet, she is since forever for him the cause come from without of an astounding explosion:

> I already wondered what was happening here, the landing in full flight or the take-off lights ablaze of an unheard-of speech, the appearance of an unidentifiable letter and literary object. What *is* this? I asked myself more or less. What is happening here? What is happening to me? What genre? Who could ever read this? Me?[19]

Naturally, there is no opposition between outside and inside, everything that happens happens only at the line of nondemarcation, at the edging, at the self's exinterior, in the outside of the inside, that doubly locked heart that he calls the secret. The event does not happen, does not arrive, it arrives only as not identifiable, it arrives a long time before itself, it arrives for the eternity that has (not) begun (un)beknownst and (nowhere) in plain sight to the designated parties, it comes to be recognized only after itself, a long time after many years after its *landing in flight*, later. To be sure right away there will be promise. And date. But what will later make of the moment an event is the endurance of the promise. It takes time, all of time. Until once again we find ourselves there. When one day this day comes back to us, it's because, having made the rounds of time, it comes back as event.

It is beyond oblivion that an unforgettable makes appearance. Something that had no name, except a borrowed one.

★

– You are *my insister*, he says to me.

This can be heard and understood only in a foreign land where we find ourselves beneath the same *Passat*, Celan would say, with the trade wind for canopy.

What pleases me no end in this word, which you give me as a present, your found object, your genius discovery, this feminine or masculine untranslatable, is that I can likewise turn it round on you. You too you are *my insister. My insisting.*

II

The Flying Manuscript

On 7 April 2005 I was in Arcachon, my Arcachon and the one in Blanchot's *Death Sentence*. I had the sad good fortune of finding again the manuscript of *Veils*, yes, the first draft, the 'very first,' blown in from very far, 'from very far,' you say, you write

'from the furthest reach possible of the truth,' you would say it seems to me, for as soon as you show yourself, in whatever form or kind or body it may be, I recognize you, one recognizes you by the veritable shower of truth, with the showering of thought from the first breath you throw us off our feet,

sad good fortune but good fortune in truth to come upon again, unexpectedly, a manuscript whose every feature leaps into view, and all the graphisms, apocalypse in the house but dazzling, I see at once everything and I see nothing

Voilà. Veils has come back!

(I am going to reread the manuscript found in a bottle I say to myself)

– One has to imagine a bottle like an airplane deprived of a pilot you say

As for you, you would write the sentence like this:

– I am going to reread the manuscript found in a bottle

– You think that you find yourself in a bottle?

– In a Klein bottle, perhaps. It is as if I am in a machine.

– Who's piloting? etc.

Who is the pilot of the pilot?

– For, in a visible, readable, spectacular way, you have always staged the entry of voices into your interior scene, pushing the interior to declare and show itself, underscoring the dissociated dialogic dimension of the I-of-me game of your 'I' caught unawares, despite your always standing guard, inscribing so many times the theater of the drama in which you are the blind man and the prophet, you, unlike me, stage the irruption of foreign forces into your course, I mean to say into your inner forum [*for*] – your own foreign forces, your own polemos, you fight with yourself. I mean to say: you fight over yourself, you tear yourself apart. And you let it be seen by the people who follows you and who looks longingly at you, and whom you call upon to witness this tearing to pieces. And to this people, an immensity, you say You, you name it and bring it toward you, with the name You.

As for me, I keep my shatterings and gaps of me sewn up in my text, embroidered in parentheses.

As for you, you pick your seams apart and pick fights with yourself, you lacerate, you take your life by the throat and throttle it, you strike blows against yourself, like a king of Greek tragedy.

Each time I say to myself: how Greek he is, and how strange that is. And then: this is due to his antiquity, to the secret origin of his very ancient being. As if his soul, his psyche had been forged at the conflictual confluence of the Judeogreek and Christian worlds, at the moment of clash that gives birth to the firstborn of the condemned-to-die, J.C. or J.D., king of the Greek Jews

(Look, for example, let us view *Veils*, let us open the still virgin book, still uncut, kept hidden by Mr Galilée's unanalyzed, instinctive wish to hand over to the reader a volume still in its chrysalis. I half-open it (yes, I confess, this copy, my copy, is intact) to page 25.[20] Here begins your chant and as I leaf through without tearing it, I see through the portal that the first act of this play is altogether controversed by your voices, up to page 40 [42]. Dispute. Cruel accounting of the stations of a cross announced by the first intratextual words in underlined characters: *Before the verdict, my verdict.*

(I'm obliged to specify *which* first words I'm talking about because, as usual, you will have multibegun,

57

opening in this way as well a little arena of rivalry between the pretenders-to-the-status-of-first-words, where at least three sorts of *vers* 'succeed' each other, each pretender situating itself in a place and behind a mask (or character situating itself in a place and behind a different mask (or character, or font), like this:

1

Sero te amaui

Toward [*Vers*] Buenos Aires, 24–29 November 1995

→ **Before the verdict, my verdict**, before, befalling me, it drags me down with it in its fall, before it's too late, stop writing.

in such a way that the three beginnings advance at the same time in the direction of a Penelope who pretends to be waiting for them at the bottom of the page.[21]

– To succeed oneself/each other [*Se succéder*], that's what awaits me, you tell me.)

Now I ask my mother the midwife 'to cut *Veils* for me.'

Now I go down to the kitchen where my mother has rung the bell. She has prepared an orange juice for me. I say very loud: you will have to cut a book for me. I say I feel good with you. She says: Me, I have disappeared completely. What are you saying? I say. She says: I'm not very visible.

I go back up toward the paper, this sheet. Who says: I am not very visible?

I say: I see you anyway.

To come back to the manuscript of *Veils*, I had forgotten the manuscript in your hand in a drawer and it came back, by itself, while I was musing around the impossible theme of this colloquium in Barcelona for which I take up the pen today

impossible theme of a very impossible colloquium almost impossible impossible to accept it impossible not to accept this invitation (you did a commentary on this in advance in *Passions*) addressed first of all, title-wise, to the two of us (of *the two of us* you did a commentary in advance in *Fourmis*)

Two words (you again!) first of all to Marta Segarra, for Marta and about Marta: *merci, merci*. Or else Alas, alas. Marta to whom you said yes I will come, I will come perhaps naturally. Or else: I will come, perhaps, naturally.

In any case, you will add this 'now-in-2003' each time, if I couldn't (can't) come, God forbid, you must do it. With me without me. For lover of the impossible you destine us, all, to the impossible.

What did I think on hearing these words? Nothing. I did a lot of nothingthinking and of trembling in the place of thinking during all those months without me [*mois sans moi*], me within me but not without you. One must very well obey, one is drowning, one grabs on to the watchword, one is obliged with the words *very well*, one drowns in obedience. One bends to your will that is hidden to yourself. You yourself obey the order given. Who gives? It can only be life. And thereupon we agree.

As for you, you think on death, all the time, I say,

– You can say that again you say –

– I mean you think on death [*tu penses à la mort*] the way you say I write on dreaming [*j'écris au rêve*]. That is to say: on the force of dreaming, under its impulsion, to its address, with its help. But you think living you think of living, to live is that, I say

– But who's talking of living! you say –

Here we go, we're starting over, once again, we shift the agreement, yet I am sure that we agree you hold on to life like no one else, you want it all totally including the end that does not exist, – I hold on to life like no one else in flesh and bone, to life in person but not the other, the unknown, here we go we start over the endless conversation that feeds on mighty and insubstantial food, phantom food in some way, refined, rich, prepared by imagination and phantasm. We speak to one another with words that sparkle and mystify, will-o'-the-wisp words. For example the word otherwise, *autrement.* The otherwise, you say, is the truth. It is not you but the other who lies [*c'est l'autre qui ment*].

So yesterday 2003 we reached an accord, you with me, to imagine a scene of conversation, as a way of outsmarting the difficulty of the theme and the time. Of diminishing fatigue if possible, by dividing it. A practice already well tested between us and that one day we'll have to talk about.

Impossible to keep one's word on this subject, the subject of the colloquium: 'The Event as Writing: Reading Cixous and Derrida Reading Each Other/Themselves' at this moment or any other, I don't see how, said I tormenting myself, these last days, how to be able, it's only barely that I can want to, but to be able to, in the state in which we are, said I to myself, half dead, and thus half alive, and no one to say which is which [*lequel laquelle*], and how to keep the word together, how in these obscure and unknown circumstances keep together word and togethering. I was twisting like two worms [*vers*] or two pieces of worm-verse

This feeling of impotence was mine, not yours, quite obviously. It is I on this earth who am laboring under the sensation of *sans.* A sensation merely, a semblance of sans, fright of the self before the new senses of all senses, weakness of my step that is learning to walk/work otherwise my impotence.

It was then that the manuscript of *Veils* made its ghostly return from out of one of my drawers where it had been sleeping utterly forgotten by me but not by the gods, quite obviously. *Voilà*, it comes back and *not just once but twice.*

The first time there is the surprise of the rediscovery eight days ago: as if I were receiving for the first time, the second first time, and a wholly other time, this manuscript that you sent me already years ago. Thanks to a breakdown in the oblivion. I made its acquaintance or took cognizance of it with sorrowful joy. All of you who are listening to me or reading me, here's the thing: you had sent me by air mail from the Aspen Towers Hotel, in the República Argentina, 30-11-95

the manuscript of *Veils*, first draft, first spurt [*premier jet*]. The manuscript of *Veils* scribbled in a jet plane above the Cordillera de los Andes. *Jet* (the last time you did the commentary of *Jet* was, I believe, in GGGG. In this text you grabbed hold of a spurt of 'jet' and of G harvested in a text of mine so as to restitch it into yours, by setting it like a grain of salt into your sea water.

I note this because your way of reading me – and not just me, of course – has always been *a fashion*/a mode of setting, as one sets a stone in a jewel, a magnifying setting, an overinsetting that your quick glance practiced first of all on the texts of Blanchot, Genet, Celan, and so forth (I cite here the texts called literary, for which you reserve an even more bejeweled, bejoyous reading than your enhancing reading of the philosophical corpus. (*Bijou* [jewel], what a word! I give it to you. It comes to us from the Breton *bizou* in 1460. I'm not joking. As a ring, the turning round of the *biz* – the finger. And, imagine this, it is said of any relatively small work in which a highly refined art is revealed . . .)

To come back to this resuscitated manuscript, I was first of all seized by joy at the apparition of the face of your handwriting. Joy, joy. The blue self-portrait on the slightly dark envelope. Secret of a face depicted on paper. Veil 24 cm × 19 cm. Joy amplified by another joy born of the feeling of rarity. For everyone knows that your works are in the vast majority, if not almost all of them, typed, done on the machine (allowing for exceptions and correspondence). Joy of the face printed for resurrection-re-edition. Joy ensorrowed as if at the sight of the Veil of Veronica. Veiled joy.

The forgotten circumstances, which obviously I remember right away, had demanded some time ago this handwritten air mail missive. It had required anguish and suffering in the air for you to make this urgent gesture, doubly urgent: (1) write very quickly and by hand. And from afar. (2) Send it right away, that is to say, turn it over to another's keeping, here mine.

(3) I add that the safekeeping intended by the missive was accompanied by a request to keep secret, secret from myself, this closed envelope slipped into an envelope and put on hold. (4) That is not all, later on I will be seen to receive still more. (5) I was obliged to make an effort, either not to cry or not to call you right away to tell you the news of this 3 April 2005.

In 1995 you put into my care the keeping of a secret envelope, a secret fold [*pli*], while recommending that I not open it, here then is the fabulous scene. There is the miraculous sail, the white one in the distance. Promise me not to open it . . . you say. Right away the strange powers that lurk in fables and myths leap up and surround us. Us: me, the secret letter, you. Veil not to be read. Veil to non-unveil. Flying, volatile letter.

Hardly do you ask me: promise, and I promise (you), naturally. I promise a blank promise. As if in blank to God. 'Inside it was prescribed to install the ark of the testimony. This veil will be *for you*, says Yahweh to Moses' (*Voiles*, 31; *Veils*, 29). Veil of separeunion. As we know only too well, the promise is full of threats. Threats of terrifying reprisals if the given word should be betrayed, to be sure. But above all indecipherable threats linked to the magic necessity of keeping secret for a period whose term can be decided only by you, by a judgment [*arrêt*] in your destiny, a sentence/arrest of life of death of life of death, a sentence that you are awaiting, that will be made known to you one day or other, and that you will make known to me in your turn in my turn an other day, whose date is still postponed. Not that you will reveal the secret to me but that, depending on the verdict, you will let me know what is to be the fate of the missive. About the verdict, one will never know the truth. All that you say about it, here, before it is handed down, and all that you know is that:

'you won't escape, even if the verdict is favorable, that is, negative' (*Voiles*, 34; *Veils*, 32).

★

What is *a verdict (that is) negative*?

Who is going to render it? A terrifying father? A judge? A jury?

For which fault – there are so many of them you say (see the list *Voiles*, 35; *Veils*, 32), perjuries, blasphemings, profanations, etc.

of which you are innocent.

In another book, you will see how, detached from the world and time, flying from hour to hour, he sends himself on white paper the following order in two lines: 'Write this from very far away, as if after life, in the lower corner, as low as possible or almost.' You will see how he addresses himself and executes to the letter. Later on I myself will find this injunction again, written 'as if after life' in the lower corner, the lowest possible in my house, or almost

I will then understand successively what I had not then understood,

'as if after life.'

All of this will have always happened as if after life – in a race by sea, by air, by mountains after life.

All life long to run after life

★

– I am asking myself today, no, suddenly *it* asks me by sinking its teeth into my heart, if that is why I had utterly forgotten this manuscript found again by the chance reshifting of a drawer. As if, no sooner the interdiction lifted then the obedience to the edict *to not* had been revived, the promise to keep closed remaining alive beyond all the events, the promise and (the) reason, or instinct.

– Promise me. – I promise you. – Do not open. – Until my return. – Until your return.

Do not open, do not read.

And naturally you repeated this injunction more than once. As if I couldn't really promise except by promising more than once and really keep and you, as if you could feel the firmness of the promiseland only after testing it with tip of your toe more than once. Interdiction, verdict, promised, a few of the words from the same fire, which we always fed with respect.

– The interdiction, I say, stokes.

– The interdiction is not a form of combustible fuel, you say. – In the sense of what makes it take I say. – It is a general law you say.

The interdiction is his daily dog

★

Never will it have been seen, I have never seen in history – never will my nuncle Freud have seen in his life – such a titanic battle against himself.

– You are a combattitant I say.

Don't go thinking, you friends who are listening to this little story, that the reiteration of the demand signified an absence of confidence in me. On the one hand, reiteration has always been a party to or at odds with the structure of the promise: the 'once and for all' has to be renewed more than once. Once a week let's say. On the other hand, if there is lack of confidence, and that is right, it is in destiny. I was posted by you in front of destiny. You needed then that we be two holding up the sail of the promise against the gale of destiny. At stake then was a verdict. At stake alreadythen [*déjalors*] was a verdict.

For this injunction not to open, I could propose more than one supposed explanation. You too imagine diverse interpretations. I will not do so. I never asked him for an explanation, never. I promised it. He reminds me: 'you didn't open it at least? – No.' This depicts the two characters. I am describing. This could be compared to many familiar models of *you not to*, Adam, Eve, Abraham, Bluebeard. But that is not it. It's something else.

Among the explanations, there is one I can give. It does not have to do with the secret: his customary reluctance to share a text that he deems to be still imperfect or not altogether brought to term. The rigor of his signature. The need to be impeccable – as much as possible. All the other explanations belong to him.

★

– Why does he send this text, enclosed in an envelope, to H.C.? Among the possible answers, here is one: we had agreed, before his departure on a distant, very distant voyage, that he would write the text promised to René Major for the issue of *Contretemps* devoted to *Veils* (thus the first take of *Veils*) setting out from, around, starting with *Savoir*, the text on which he desired to prop up the fatigue – he talks about it in an almost desperate tone, everyone will have heard it quite well – caused by the veil persecution –

It was the first time that you sent me an envelope not to be opened so long as and until –

That it was indeed the first time I was not sure. I might have thought it was the only and the last –

It comes back to me today that the same scene took place one other time. It was in May 2003. You were returning from a faraway trip. In front of you the announcement of a trip without fixed harbor, without measure. You had written for a colloquium devoted to the archives I deposited at the BN, which was supposed to take place at the end of that May, a text whose title you tell me. This time it is deposited into my hands that you 'send,' from a wholly other great distance, this text written from a very distant interior, in a closed envelope. Not to be opened. Except and unless. I promised. More than once you call me and you say: you didn't open it at least. This scene depicts us. I swear to you I haven't touched it. – Oh if only I could believe you!

It's not that he doesn't trust me. It is in believing that he has difficulty believing. This time it seemed to me I could guess the reasons for which I was not to open. This text in his absence.

– How is it going to be possible to translate this sentence? You worry about the translators. On the one hand. On the other you take great pleasure in dribbling around translation. That's why you keep watch on the little football player in you.

I didn't open the envelope.

How would I have opened it?

With a knife, you will say to me, in your equivocal guise.

★

My mother comes into the study with a large kitchen knife in her hand. It is for *Veils*.

– Why do you say that you are not visible? I say.

– Because we're not seeing a lot of each other here. Maybe you're the one who is not visible.

– Maman? I say.

– You are inspired? She smiles. She cuts the book. She smiles.

– I love it that you're here.

– Like the cats.

I look at her. I look at her visibility. For a long time.

Two different visibilities, you say.

I see what you mean, yes.

Two different visibilities. And two different non-visibilities. Some day I will talk about your present visibility, the one to which I am applying myself and at which I am employed, 'au-dedans de moi,' as you say in *Rams*, in that 'inner forum [*for intérieur*] that never closes' as you say (p. 19) and where you are as always at once the strongest, that is, *the most fort* and the most *da*.

'Au-dedans de' is an expression of yours. As for me I usually use 'en moi' to say 'within me.' You are the one who is right. *Au-dedans* is more interior and more sheltering than *en*.

She has finished. – I will try to read it a little, this book, says my mother.

She gets up. The knife.

– Me with this butcher knife. It gives me the willies.

This butcher knife, I say to myself, in order to cut *Veils*, I'll tell you about it.

★

When you gave me the not to be opened envelope before the BN colloquium, I didn't remember the first envelope.

★

The *second coming back* of the manuscript took place a few days later, when I arrived in April 2005 at my writing house where I went on your order as given in 2003: 'If I can't go to Barcelona, it will be necessary [to go] all the same.' Absolute order and without commentary. Order without authority.

For months I have been thinking about it like a poor beast being led to the impossible. I have no tricks in me, only anguished submission.

I can describe in broad strokes my interior state concerning this ordeal: there's anguish that swirls and whirls and will never end – (neither in my life nor with my death, in my opinion) concerning the For [*Pour*], your famous double-doored For, the one that offers and the one that takes back and substitutes. Instead of spreading out the load, the weight, as hoped, here I am summoned by fate to keep the word for your apparent silence or the appearance of your silence, having to keep impossibly account of the different kinds of absence, presence, the presence of absence, knowing full well that there is no absolute absence, only presences made of different stuff, with different thicknesses, solidities, endurance, stability, tangibility. How not to betray! Oh! Translate, you, the depth of my anguish. I know that you hear me and that you are unhappily unhappy. And if I know such an apparently mysterious thing, it is not because I am a mystic or inspired (which I am, but that would not suffice) as my mother says, inspired, but it's because I know you a little and that having never ceased suffering *for* the other his and her whole life, you continue.

'Don't be sad.' These are words you addressed to all those whom you love, so seriously, and so often. – You too, don't be sad.

Cruel saddening sadness, which saddles every feeling of tenderness.

'Don't be sad' you say. That's just like you. How not to obey you? I mean: not to disobey you?

But you when I say to you: 'forget,' you point out that this cannot happen on command. Don't forget, you say to me. You are in command. Thereupon we argue over the you the who, the how of the command, we co-mandate one another. Words words.

We observe their motives, their movement. They are never still, they never die.

★

Mystique. The word *mystique* takes hold of him. For example one day in 1989, a certain use of the word mystical, in whose vicinity, nosing around, he meets up with Pascal, Montaigne.

Mystical: this is authority, the foundation of authority. No reason can be given! That's the way it is. This word mystical, now he's pleased, Jacques Derrida, when he *plays* with this word. What does it mean, what will one say of this play? Philosophically?

A playful vein, played out in words, circulates through all his philosophy. Philosophy always in translation.

Two words regarding words. Words between us – often German words. *Les bons mo*ments in his philosophical work are always word moments. The bad words can also be good. But there is an interdiction on evil words: one must evoke them from a distance and beware pronouncing them.

There are words of power, magic words, passwords. There are *bons mots* – there are the two-words. I am going to have to write the book of words, next year. There will be a chapter on the word *portée*. *Portée* in French. And a chapter on the word *porter* [to carry, to bear] in German – *tragen* – *tragen* is a preferred word. He takes it from Heidegger's ear. The extraordinary play that he, Heidegger, practices on the word *tragen*. Derrida's ecstasy: *Ausgetragenes Kind*. To bear and to bring into the world. To carry the voice of the friend in oneself, *bei sich tragen*. To bear something within that is not self. That is different. This, this is me with him. But as for him, Proteus Derrida, he bears in him something that is the one who is his antagonist, himself his adversary, his other, his double double: at once prophet and persecutor. *Portée des mots, Protée des mots*, the import of words, Proteus of words twenty times.

He adds them up and tells me the story of *tragen*, in 1988 for example, in 1995. One cannot imagine the ancientness and the import of certain words.

★

The word *möglich* for example – its secret powers
How not to obey you! If I can. Can I? Might I?

I am inhabited by the enormous force of the *Unmöglichkeit*. This is the word that comes to me. I bless it: it is one of the words around which we have sojourned. I'll come back to it later. I hear Omi my grandmother crying out often: '*das ist ja unmöglich.*' How to communicate to you the accents, the exclamativity, the tonicity of the language and the body, in German, the idiomaticity, the supplement of *ja* the hammering of the *un*, the sigh? I communicate it to you over the telephone. I imitate Omi. I sound out for you all the marvelous and German reserves merely in the semantic family of *mögen*. You, with your super-philosophical ear your philosophic nose, your taste, your zophic refinement, you have guessed, with all your senses, eight, ten – more perhaps, by reading Heidegger, Eckhart or Angelus Silesius, that this *mögen* has unheard-of resources, inaudible in translation.

★

You dig, you drill, you raise the stakes.

You call me: – How would you translate *mögen*? *Vermögen*?

I switch into German. *Ich möchte gern*, I rediscover it while slipping you these so very subtle idiomatic connotations that cause to melt into one another the verbs to want/to will to be able to to savor, that mix and only on the German tongue the taste of self and the taste of the object. I would like to know how far you are going to be able to go (still) further in French.

— *Mögen?* That's to want or to will and to be able to, to have the power [*vouloir et pouvoir*]. What do you want to know? says my mother. It is: difficult to translate. It is: to be able to do something one wants to do but that one is not sure of being able to do. I would really like to be able to translate *mögen*. My sister and I *wir könnten ausgehen, aber wir mögen es nicht* says my mother. There is always an uncertainty, with Eri, always.

Ich mag das nicht, says Eri says my mother, something that you eat, it means you don't like it. That, that's Eri. I don't like this, I don't like that. — *Ich möge das gern*, that means we like that. *Wir mögen das nicht*, it's not to our liking.

Das ist unmöglich, it's impossible, it's not at all possible a hundred percent. *Das ist möglich*, it's possible, not 100% out of a hundred.

— Where is the willing or wanting in *Unmöglichkeit?*

— *Unmöglich?* There's nothing to be done! — *Ganz unmöglich*, it's utterly impossible.

Möglich, it seems possible

— And *Vermögen?* the verb — It means that I want nearly. I could but it's not obligatory, there's a possibility, says my mother. *Das Vermögen*: that's possession.

When you have money. *Das kostet ein Vermögen*: it's
going to cost a fortune, says my mother.

– *Es ist ja unmöglich*: so it's impossible. It's a word that
allows several possibilities, you see. *Es könnte möglich
sein, neh?* It could be possible, huh.

You need this word?

– Not me, Jacques Derrida.

– It's not possible. *Das Wort ist wirklich unmöglich.*

Ob er mögt oder nicht

It's really an elastic word says my mother, over-
whelmed.

Ich mag nicht, it's not to my liking.

★

This *mögen* enchants him, in the middle of work on
Pardon, Perjury, Hospitality, here it comes to the surface,
used by Heidegger in the sense of to desire, love. What
a delightful amazement. This *Letter on Humanism*, this
thing, he had read it I don't know how many times in
the last forty years, and it's the first time he notices
what Heidegger's doing, and him too, with the word
possible, he pulls it very far in that direction, to desire,
love.

It's difficult for French people to work on
Möglichkeit, vermögen, power, to be able to, the faculty
of being able to, one must be able to. A power
close to authorization also to the possibility *given*, it

enchants him to be able to discover after forty years a word that he is going to be able to be able to make work in French. And to have missed it for forty years. *Felix culpa*, it moves him to have received the message, with delay, which is how it has to be. You would think it was life, you would think it was love, you would think this too late, this toolateness or toolateo'clock, that makes the scales of time swing back, swing ahead. Fortunately everything is written, there is no too-late in reading. It is never too late, in the present that comes back, constant, to present itself to reading. We take this expression 'it is never too late': by seasoning it with a little amazement it begins to be able to say something other than what one might think. One never gets bored with Heidegger, he says, a guy who pays attention to what he says, he laughs. – With Heidegger-text. The other one, the Black Forest one, the dullard with the hand-knit socks, you don't like him at all.

– One never gets bored with any Jacques Derrida, I say. It is the able-to-pay-attention to what you say that excludes boredom.

Let's take *ennui* [boredom], I say. Here we are at the dictionary. *Inodiare. Ennui* barely hides odium, hatred. One never feels hatred with someone who pays attention to what he says. On one side, that of the speaking, this is so true: the guy who pays attention to what he says is someone who pays attention to the other; to where he puts his words down. Carefulness, compassion, love. On the other side, nothing guarantees that some *odium* of resentment is not brewing in the secret of those who have no love for attention.

The one who awakens words, who attracts attention to attention, the one who weighs his words (you say: 'I am weighing my words,' then you weigh that expression and the word 'to weigh') attracts as well, for good and for ill, love and hatred. It's because he shows, teaches, learns, takes the pain, to read. To take pains to live. Learn to take pain in order to live. At the same time read everything (in other words: see to and provide for reading, seeing, writing, thinking) go seek and receive, let come what you ended up calling with a vastly hospitable word: the event.

Surmission and submission. The two together.

★

I would so like to be able to want to be capable of the impossible say I to myself. It will be necessary all the same that I might. I sense very well (I *sense* sans knowing sans certainty sans presumption) I sense very well that if you cannot 'come' to Barcelona nothing prevents you from being there: There is no limit or boundary to the suppleness of being.

★

It's raining. I am writing on this rainy Wednesday 2005. I hear your voice. Where? How? Clearly. Internally. It is a Wednesday in the month of March 2001. Clearly internally. You pronounce one of *your* sentences, one of those sentences signed J.D., without peer without equivalent one of your untranslatables: '*Comment voulez-vous que je meure?*' you say.

A real find. Another one of your feats I say, a defeated feat you say, I'm blown off my feet I say you dare to wave *le fichu* [the rag, the scarf, but also the guy who is done in, done for, finished] in front of a room of listeners an incredible provocation to thinking, to spend oneself un-thinking, to sacrifice, threaten reassure, defiance of mastery, admonishment of the need for meaning, you go fate one better. Fate: *Pour* in Hebrew.

You have just sent fate to its fate, played one of your turns on *for*, that is, *pour*, rimmed round the *pour*, this French *pour* whose disseminal opening you brought to the fore, a pourple dissemination, blood red. On this Spring day of 2001, a seminar Wednesday, you say: 'if one day I knew what *pour* means perhaps then I could [*pourrais-je*] die while beginning to think what is happening to me [*ce qui m'arrive*].'

Everything you say is under the care of *if* [*tout ce que tu dis est sous* si].

80

How do you want me to die? / How can I be expected to die? / How ever can I die? you say to the people who follow you. You say these terrible and scintillating things to your seminar, you throw them into the balance, you oscillate them above the heads of your listeners, you flex them between care and care-free, impossible to take you literally – what did he say? what are you saying? – everything is literal but under the seal of perhaps, everything that is stirred up is sent back, you say to sow terror. That is what you do: you sow terror. The sower sows. The sower so loves himself and weeps for himself, in advance, you are so far out ahead, you want and you do not want to be wept over, you want you cannot not want not to be lost one second from view, from hearing when you sketch out in the distance the sequence for which you want to push thought to the summit or to the extremity of thought: 'die while beginning to think what is hap-pening to me,' that is what you'd like to give yourself, *du möchtest*, if you could if it was up to you, as one said.

Only you do not say only this, which already sur-passes or surpossibles itself. To the same you say: – *Comment voulez-vous que je meure?*

To the same you say: how is it possible for me to die? This will never happen to me. Rest assured. If you are afraid. Except if. Unless. Even as you say to them in the same breath: 'In what way do you want me to die?

Oh, yes, yes, I know very well that you want what you do not want, or vice versa, the death drive circulates beneath love's floor, choose the pain or punishment you wish, that you wish for yourselves in wishing it for me. I hear what you do not say, I hear what you do not know that you want, I hear that you cannot want, what you do not want to want I hear it. I am not a magician. Love is like that all mixed up with dying, at least most of the time. Like birth. The newborn with some meconium on the tongue, that is what we are.

'As for me, I do not want to die. It is for you that I would surrender myself perhaps, if I succeeded in knowing what *pour* means to say to me. Testimony or response to tortuous love

Love, I tell you, love, since the time I have been telling it to you − (remember my seminar on testimony) he says to each and every one of his breathless people − is it not impregnated or else does it not have the tint of a desire for death tinted with a desire for life, or vice versa and you who love me as I love me do you not want me also to say yes to what you are letting me hear? You follow me?'

One hears his voice, it is raining. He is always worrying about the other.

How do you want me to die!/ How can I possibly die! he says to the people who are following him, and who open up and split themselves into more than one part, depending on whether one hears or doesn't hear the *pour* turning in one sense or in the other.

It is springtime this evening, once again you make the rounds of the year, it is year one, the first or the second of a century, yours

– You're playing again to win, who's for winning, *qui pour gagne*, I say to you – Kippor did you say? – But how do you expect, how can you want anyone to translate you? you say – And you? I say. Do you want it? How? How much? To read you? You who set spinning all texts. All Testes. All Heads. Who else, in the whole French language, will have ever been capable of throwing out such a sentence? You really stuck it to us that day [*Tu t'es bien fichu de nous*]. I can still hear it, I can still hear you that day, crying up your sleeve and smiling at the disarray you will have sown in the heart of your hermeneuts. One day like another. One other day like each of your days. Nothing special. Every day is perhaps this day that is perhaps the day If [*le jour Si*].

When I cite this giant of an unsigned sentence to my daughter with the philosophical ear, her voice says to me: 'Derrida would be speaking of a kind of generalized homonymy.' He alone would say this sentence, from out of his uninterrupted solitude, he, in his solitude, would say: 'how do you want me to die / how

83

can I possibly die.' One might then hear resonating Blanchot's complaint mixed with the fear and the pain of Jacques Derrida. Who is capable of death? Such a thing is not possible. You mean who wants death. Not me. No, it is the other who has the responsibility for my death, the desire of my fear.

'He alone' this Sentence would say. He alone, so haunted by the other, by I don't know whom, who forlorns him even more.

– I am listening to you, I say, I listen to your thought weave itself.

– You know how to hear yourself, you say.

– You think? Me, I think it's you on the brink that I hear [*Moi je crois que c'est toi en croix que j'entends*].

So we scandalize ourselves the one the other

– I don't know how it can be translated, you worry, into French. All of these nested settings.

I have a conventional pedagogical concept. When I see the difference between your text and mine! In the lecture mode, for the ones who are a little slow, I fish them out because I'm a pedagogue, whereas you, you cut them loose.

– *You*'re the one saying that?! (pronounce this reply with all intonations, interrogative, exclamatory, etc.)

And *he*'s the one, the almost disappeared vibratory one according to the play of his speech (you will have recognized a little Mallarmé 'on a subject'), who really got us with his tricky sentence from 21 March 2001, *he*'s the one who finds *me* disconcerting. What if he were right?

★

I'm thinking of his way of struggling on the subject of truth. How he equivocates himself. Dodges and feints himself.

We make another round of the year, it's our eternal dispute that needs to wind up its merry-go-round each one his hobbyhorse, you claim that mine is called Life, I assert that Life is yours, you say to me Death or Debt [*Mort ou Mors*] one can never tell, it's a circus, the one of *Circumfession*, the thirteenth round or the first, anguished he turns around the bed of his mother with compassion, with a desolate circoncupiscence for the belief of the 'believers in days of old' I have already told you so many times, but nothing appeases it, he envies those who were tranquil in the knowledge that they were going to be reunited – in paradise – Marguerite's aunt and uncle in Belgrade – in paradise – how happy they were in days of old you don't doubt it?

– I have already told you – You believe? – Yes I believe. Paradaysofold. I believe I believe – Ha! you see. Future centuries. You really believe in that? Tell me – On earth?

The merry-go-round whirls.

– That it is not interrupted. That there will still be some me that will be me. The only interruption, in life, death in life. One can die only in life, not in death. To be killed, in the fullness of life.

– Have to have already renounced the me in its absolutely mortal singularity in what will no longer have any trace. To merge into an alterity. But the little me that says me me me.

– There has to be someone to keep alive. We'll talk about it again in ten years, in 2001.

★

With each death of a loved one, with each life that passes we make the round of belief in place

I am running [*cours*] in place today he says, mail, mail, mail [*courrier, courrier, courrier*]

My father lives in me, I say. And his little me? he says. His great me in me I say. Do you realize, if I forgot? I would then make him die.

– In me my father still lives, I say.

This kind of life gives him a lot to think about.

– I remember very well he says the day of my sister's son's Bar Mitzvah, my father. He said: I'm done for [*je suis fichu*]. I remember very well this memory.

Our merry-go-round, ageless you say, young, I say. It could be called circumversation or circum-version.

Me, he says, 'I keep forever reminding her . . . that we die in the end, too quickly. And I always have to begin again' he says in June 1998 at Cerisy.[22] And I always have to begin again reminding/remembering it.

Right after reading his *Portrait as Young Jewish Saint*, that is to say my Portrait: from the beginning between us the question of French, the common gesture regarding the French language, a kind of effraction

The gesture that we make together differently together

★

I listen to him, telephonidiomatically. Since our debut. *Debut* what a word! Everything began by ear. With a certain music of French, no one in the world *speaks* like that, I said to myself, no one signs, marks *speech* in such a strong way. Since forever I have been listening to his second nature. 'Nature' according to Jacques Derrida. His 'as for's,' his '*quant à*,' his cantata always already there. Whereas in my case paper is required for the sentence to take shape. I need the skin, the body, right hand on the body to tame the chaos into a sentence. To trap the most fugitive words.

He remarks the word 'trap.' You use it all the time. He catches me at it. He traps me. He pays close attention to what I say. (We talk a lot about hunting and fishing, have you noticed?) – I hadn't noticed. Now this word is marked remarked, I try to avoid it, it catches up with me elsewhere, it betrays my dreams. Then I ask myself why I am trying to flee what he remarked. I fall upon the word *remark*. His word. And that of my paternal grandmother. She made remarks to me. I feel myself remarked? Yet another swipe of the paw by the cat deconstruction. Remarked is good and it is not good. I chase away the cat the way one chases away a fly. I now no longer know if I'm fleeing or pursuing I mean desiring his remark.

He snares, I trap, he fishes out

I admit it, I trap, I track, words. For him instead it's *vocables*, have you noticed that?

– Why do you say 'vocable' so often? Me, never. You right away with *The Origin of Geometry*, you initiate it and probably much earlier. It's with *The Origin* that I remarked it I remember. Your vocablation. Your vocation, your vocabulation

He likes this word in voices, a little scholarly, a little singerly

– I am (following) the worm/verse, he says, who with several vocables, makes a new word [*mot nouveau*] foreign to the language and as if incantatory.

I did not say *total* on purpose, and I didn't say *neuf* either. Total is not of his thinking. *Nouveau* provides us [*nous vaut*] with a supplement of sense, he 'knows how.'

★

I am (following) the Worm, the Ver . . .

It's been six pages since I announced the *second return* of the manuscript of *Veils*. You thought maybe I had forgotten, lost the thread. I was merely delaying, without doing it on purpose but not unwittingly, just as there is a suspension as soon as it is a question of *Verdict*: one wants and doesn't want to receive the message. Him, you know what he's like, in this case he says: '*Pardon de ne pas vouloir dire*' [Pardon for not meaning/wanting to say].

Yet another homonymic sentence that would require a chapter of explanation. But I will not do that. I want to turn to this Return. The manuscript in his hand is spread on my desk, to my right, I hear it breathing. I am coming . . .

★

Just two more words that he will have confided to me that Spring 2001 when he was acting out the fateful scene, in his seminar. It was a question of the *Verdict*, Kafka's, *Das Urteil*, a dark tale, example of mortal auto-immunity. I was reminding him of its meanders. For me it is once again Georg my father who gets himself suicided by the other his internal and external father. I know this horror by heart. The last blow, the last page,

89

would be a premonitory version of *États d'âme de la psychanalyse*. It is a magical 'suicide.' You are killing me. Georg *eats* and *drinks* death, his death, with an insane appetite. To please his father. He dies for him. He lets himself fall off a bridge. During this time, on page 9 of *États d'âme*,[23] he makes the personal pronouns and the semantic variations of the verb 'to suffer' turn around the word 'cruelly.' It is suffering, hurting everywhere. It's too much.

In diesem Augenblick ging über die Brücke ein geradezu unendlicher Verkehr.

– Me, says Jacques Derrida, the act of falling off a bridge in my car is one of my most recurrent phantasms.

– So I answer him: . . .

And he answers me: . . .

Everything is in his books.

★

– Have I finished digressing?

How not to digress? And what is more why not digress? There are many illustrious examples of digressers Sterne, Diderot, Stendhal, Freud, Jacques Derrida. You, you even begin with digression. 'First digression, in confidence,' you say to the Estates General of Psychoanalysis. True and droll 'incipit' as they say. One knows all about your 'confidences,' they are addressed to each one of everybody. Not that you are making fun of everybody and each one. But it's to recall the structural division of every me, the implacable, cruel destinerrancy. Not that you don't make fun a little of everything and everyone, including yourself. All the fatalist Jacques's are digressers, Jacques is even the proper name of every deconstructor.

Does the Digress have an end?

Life is a digression. All of literature is digressions. Mallarmé's *a flower* is a *volubilis*, the wordy French name of the morning glory. You would say: one must very well digress. One day we invent the verb *digre*. Digre me a little, you say. It is not a fated necessity, however. The straight-arrow sentence, the line, also knows you.

But digressing, traditional French usage does not like. That's understandable. We are descartized.

You will have said 'First digression, in confidence . . .' it was a gift, a wink to the thousand psychoanalysts who had come in the hope of knowing if you would know who is capable of death and what death is capable of. Next must come the second digression, at least so one believes, on the promise of these first words. Will anyone have found it? One has to imagine the faithful and assiduous reading going through this book listening to this address of genius right to the end, a reading left behind, thrown off course, dragged on to 'indirect paths,' the 'other paths' cleared by Freud, and henceforth recognized, translated, reinscribed by Jacques Derrida, carried beyond knowledge, beyond the foreseeable, launched into the space of undecidability with the energy of this *Indirektheit* in which he, Jacques Derrida, revives the value overlooked by Freud of *irrectitude*, a 'non-straightness' or 'non-rightness,' virtue and *virtus* uncovered in live action, at the quick of the subject, by the force of his soul at the dawn of the century and named with a new name. An active non-straightness (which does not mean non-passive) active even while passive, acting affectively, not subjected either to good or evil, guided only by the bound. To bound outside the circle of assassins, Kafka would say. But this is not easy when we carry our assassins within ourselves. To bound beyond the beyond, you say, toward a life other than possible life you say, this can be imagined even found, but not hoped-for. The only good [*bon*] is the bound. The leap into ethics that blows ethics sky-high. This is the gift that he would like to make us, at the end of this speech, the end of this meditation and this century, in passing, if he could make it without making it, by magic, by almightiness: the gift of *discontinuous* indirection. But he can want to make this gift but he cannot make it. He can wish to do so, he can wish it for us. Wish it for himself.

But none can give this gift, none can command it. This gift gives itself, is given, it happens that someone may have this gift, it will have been granted one knows not when or by whom, where, attributed but not with a traceable heritage. One can imagine it, one must at least try to imagine it. That is what he does.

★

At the close of the first digression, appears the one he calls 'originary affirmation,' the one who comes forward on its own, her own, and he glimpses its promise as of a land in advance, before, and beyond, transparent (he would say 'spectral') rootless, aerial, *departing from* which (and he underscores *departing from* [à partir], an affirmation of the departing-from, for one does not arrive there, as soon as it is given it gives departing from) 'a thinking of life is possible,' a 'living on.' That is his dream.

★

I said 'at the close of the first digression' which is also the close of this deeply moving, encouraging, discouraging book. It is time: the lecture lasts a time that you will not have been able to exceed beyond a certain excess. And to think that you announced that you would propose to *begin* by responding to the soul-states (those of psychoanalysis, and yours) once the digression was finished, at least seven times (beginning on page 15 [241]: 'But before I begin, assuming that I ever

93

begin . . .' Followed by page 31 [250]. 'Still before beginning, I will start off again, now on another foot.'

Interrupting myself at this point, having hardly begun, I would like, I said, to salute the Estates General of Psychoanalysis.

Why give thanks to some Estates General of Psychoanalysis? . . ..[24]

I don't know, to begin with, what, which title, or who authorizes me – certainly not myself – to salute, as I have just done, while thanking them, something like the Estates General of Psychoanalysis.[25]

Here then, in another form, is the question of the principle and thus of the beginning, namely, the inaugural act that is supposed to produce the event . . .[26]

In the end, you will not have had the time to begin, but this you knew in advance. What does it matter. It is the before-there and the beyond-there of the beyond-there that interest us. Toward which you will have indirected us, by loosening the vice of judgments that make us suffer cruelly. Cruelty, what is it? Where does it begin? Where does it end? Thought? Life?

★

But how long can one postpone?

(Here I am up to page 501 '(I have not yet left Grenoble . . .)' notes Stendhal in his Life, the one of H.B. He suspects that he derives some benefit there. I am leaving Grenoble. I return later to the second return of the manuscript of *Veils*.)

In the meantime Jacques Derrida's texts have proliferated around me, the one calling to the other.

★

Dozens of sketchpads, notepads, books disorder themselves, countless witnesses of the long path unfolding from text to text. In text-à-text, forty years.

This overabundance fills me with despair. I must multiply my life by, say, ten, no say a hundred and ten and still more, in order to attempt to keep alive your worlds of thoughts of words of sentences it's impossible humanly impossible, one must tend toward the superimpossible, I have always attempted it, to attempt to tend, to tend to attempt is the minimum.

I add four levels of work to my desk. I pile Pelion on Ossa on Babel on Moriah. Still more. I add the two cats Philia and Aletheia my autobiographical faber animals.

Magis. More. Magic?

Why not? If I too were a cat, like you have been, by your own admission, what would I do with these mountains, trees, grottos of paper? I am Aletheia. She rummages. Exhumes. Rushes all around. Suddenly reappears the manuscript. This time, I am going to enter into communication with the revenant.

★

This is perhaps always the way it is, as may be verified by consulting *Hamlet*, Act I. First they receive the figure who comes back like a shock. The second time they want to know more about it. Or as may be verified by analyzing the taste of the madeleine, first one *takes* the sip, tastes it, sucks it [*le suce*] – 'Although I didn't know yet [*ne susse pas encore*], Proust writes (– he writes *suce* and *susse*) – and had to put off until much later learning why this memory made me so happy' (*Du côté de chez Swann*, Folio 47) – one trembles, one has received a message from a dead one, the past, it is hidden, says Proust (the passed one, the dead one) 'in some material object, (in the feeling that this material object would give us) that we do not suspect. It depends on chance that we encounter this object before dying, or that we don't encounter it' (*Du côté de chez Swann*, Folio 44).

But no sooner had the sip, mixed with the crumbs of the cake, touched my palate than a shiver ran through me and I stopped, intent upon the extraordinary thing that was happening in me. A delicious pleasure had invaded me, something isolated, with no suggestion of its cause. And at once it made life's vicissitudes indifferent to me, its disasters inoffensive, its brevity illusory, in the same way that love operates, by filling me with a precious essence; or rather this essence was not in me, it was me. I had ceased to feel mediocre, contingent, mortal.

It is thus that, coming out of the drawer, I encountered before dying the face of the manuscript, the shape of Jacques Derrida's hand, whose living presence I had forgotten in the oblivion. I saw at first only the face. It never occurred to me to *read* this treasure. I contemplated the hand. I halted death. This essence of presence was in me. It was me. Up to the day when –

★

– not that I am in search of lost time, but impelled by the question that is awaiting me in Barcelona on the subject of reading, of the adventure and the event of reading between us, Jacques Derrida and Hélène Cixous

– I go back over the published, manifest texts, where one is reading the other explicitly. It is then, in the second stage, that I begin to read at a glance then slowly page 1 of the manuscript, as if for the first time, thus for the first time. Had I ever read it? already read it? When will I have read it? When will you have given me permission to open the envelope? Here is the page. Notice that it is not called *Veils*.

It is not yet called *Veils*. Nor *Le Ver à soie*.

Look at it closely. It is to be seen, you see that: it is drawn at least as much as written, it is drawritten, a breathless self-portrait. One sees the breath, one sees the wind push the sail, rush the fabric (*tissu*, one of his beloved words, that issued him forth from texts, textiles and textguiles in all genders) toward the Orient and toward the north, I would write a book to de-pict or re-picture this painting with its quivering signs that look like they've been hurled from a brush, with its letters changed into the beatings of wings, of lashes, of see's minutely sown with living punctuations, of highly eloquent silences

Look at this portrait from left to right, from top to bottom, it can also be read vertically like a poem – which it secretly is. One would have to be able to respect the modest will of the scribe, to remain faithful to the exact alignment

For example to follow the first words of each line: *écrire/qui/soit/depuis/messie/vérité/dévoilement/une autre figure/autre figure/quelqu'un/ ou mort/fin* [to write/that/

might be/from/the messiah/truth/unveiling/another figure/other figure/someone/or dead/end].

Or to note the last line of the first 'stanza,' that is to say, the last verse,

just as later, eight years or eight poems later, he will have done a reading of a Celan poem, grabbing hold instinctively of the last verse. *Die Welt ist fort, ich muß dich tragen*, this verse made forever immortal for having been read, invoked, gathered, lifted up, raised praised by your artist's love –

the last 'verse,' then, in these savage psalms hurled at the sky in the vicinity of Buenos Aires, an elevated protest, rage against the theateningness of a Verdict. The Verse before or after the original worm-*ver*, the first and the last, here it is:

fin de l'histoire – et sans linceul.
[end of history – and without shroud.]

And it is not finished, it is not final.

Within reach of these words he fires an arrow charged with raging momentum by all appearances.

Where does the arrow lead us?

To the other side, of the page, of the map, of the world, of history –

of time,

beyond time, if that could exist, in a virgin time, a virgin, virgin time oh! might you *hear* this lost sigh, exhaled confided on the *verso* of a page then once more on the verso of the following page sigh permitted, free to express the excess of the soul's suffering, since for the moment this suspiring, expiring text owes nothing to anyone, it is addressed only to him, Jacques Derrida, in detachment from himself, neither on the earth nor not-on the earth, in an airplane, between good airs and bad airs,

in this debtless moment between two times in-between, he can cry out for himself, launch the accusation or the reproach and the word of exhaustion − enough! enough! −

Enough of inheriting. Enough is always already too much. There is no enough.

Enough! it's always *enough of inheriting*, isn't it. He can't take it anymore. He doesn't want any more. Of inheriting (and therefore of giving to inherit). Of this malediction − it's like a derivative from Derrida − *D'héritage* − this repetition compulsion of debt, of owing the truth, of ancient veritage, headstrong, of immemorial, congenital condemnation, to an overdue dues, to a payment for sin decreed since time began. It's a veritable explosion of revolt in the airplane. And no one there to know it. No one to hear him crying out Enough. He cries, into the air. In the very direction of God while he tells himself He does not exist − No God, remains the *Vers*, Verse, in the very direction of the Toward. He cries toward *Vers*, in verse, he cries vermiformally, like a worm, inaudible cry, the silky cry of a self, knowing, like any reader of Rilke, from the first Duino elegy, that there is perhaps no angel who would hear him, *wenn ich schrie* – 'if I cried.' If ever he cried out, the cry annulled by the indifference or the deafness of the angel. So he can cry out, a vain cry an immense cry, alone in the white of a vain sky. To cry, not to cry, pray, not to pray. To cry: to pray, without response.

Crying didn't start yesterday, this inscribed cry of Jacques Derrida this philosophical rage, its rumblings may be heard in all his texts of revolt against fated indebtedness, accounts to be settled, against the ineluctable contamination of love – even by evil, against the condemnation to suffer from sorrow until death

And no one to hear him cry out with this naked, shaking cry, fortunately. Fortunately no one. For if someone had heard it, he would have felt guilty yet again, one more time, for having been the cause of someone's concern or worry, whoever the person might have been who was witness to his pain. He cries, and he sends me this cry enveloped in some paper, from Buenos Aires advising me not to receive it before it/he has been extinguished, the cry. I read it therefore only extinguished. Cryore.

To tell the truth: I read it not. I so much read it not that it is upon this rainy April that I read it, 'for the first time,' that I listen to it absolutely, this cry-sigh, kept vibrant, and perfectly audible, for a cry starts up again like a flame, as soon as it is kindled with a loving gaze.

I am not deaf. I believe I am able to say (NB: '*je crois pouvoir dire*' is an idiomatic formulation, derridiomatic my shrewd daughter would say, one of those possibilities of French that he is fond of, a double infinitive, even better: *si je pouvais croire pouvoir dire*, if I were able to believe I am able to say) that he dictated me and inculcated me I believe I am able to say it in the somewhat desperate hope of moderating the worrisome commotion of my temperament. I here surrender (1) to his deserved admonishment, (2) and to the pleasure of believing being able to say that I almost always heard him cry out and at the same time hold back his indignation, out of consideration for others. So as to cause the least possible suffering

I believe I am able to say as well that more than once, guessing from the rhythm of my breathing that I was hearing him and listening to him, with my whole heart in truth, he called me an 'angel' to my great detriment. For we knew too well, he as much as I – from whom he asked again for the exact quotation from the second Duino elegy – that every angel is terrible – *Jeder Engel ist schrecklich*

– Ängstlich? Or *Schrecklich? – Schrecklich.*

Schrecklich, that's terrible. Like him I could have done without this terrible being.

Und dennoch, weh mir, ansing ich euch (fast tödliche Vögel der Seele), wissend um euch.

Weh mir and *weh dir*, sometimes one needs a messenger all the same, knowing that this always points to the limit of misfortune, therefore to misfortune.

In that strange autumn of the year 1995 I therefore received a double message that was a little *schrecklich*: the-text-not-to-be-read. And the readable message that constituted the sending of this casketed text, and that painted indirectly and directly the state of a soul in danger. Was I anxious? I do not know which gods or signs prevented me then from being anxious otherwise than in solidarity.

To be sure the closed mailing signified: 'if something were to happen . . .'

I can say here that at the time I didn't believe it, I didn't believe in some fatal outcome at the end of this trip in the New World (Buenos Aires-Santiago de Chile-Valparaiso-Sao Paolo).[27]

'If something were to happen . . .' is a familiar thought in his internal forum, but he does not finish the sentence, naturally.

He was awaiting a verdict.[28]

I have to reread *Veils*, say I to myself. This immense text (I merely have to glance, for example at page 68

103

[70], randomly, to glimpse its extraordinary scope) I admit to myself not having 'so to speak' read it. And why? And how? How did I 'succeed' in not reading it except so to speak in my absence, absent-mindedly?

I who read all Jacques Derrida's texts, with at least three readings that I could name, just before, at the time, just after publication, then at least thirty times I read, each text, in front of and with my researcher friends, in our seminars, from year to year. Except for *Veils*?

As if I had failed, refused, not dared, not thought, had failed to want to dare to think – or else – *to look, to touch*, touch with my eyes this text that touches, especially in the form of the tallith, whose veils and sails rise above every reader, this tallith, summary and extension of all linens or garments and of every modeling of skin, sailcloth of life and of death this text that touches on touching, on the touched, on the question of touch, by unfurling itself as a tallith inseparable from the body 'like a memory of the circumcision' (*Voiles*, 68; *Veils*, 70). As if I had stood before the memory, the circumcision, the body, the carnal and spiritual metonymy of life death woven into that prayer shawl at a respectful distance in an alarmed restraint, an animal alarm,

dazzled. Having felt or sensed the *sacred* presence of your being in its absolute singularity, all the nearer, in

104

appearance, in that it comes from very far, from the furthest in yourself that you murmur this text of a still unheard-of genre, prophecy, prayer, revelation of an indecipherable secret, and declaration of love, to this utterly unique sublime being, your tallith the unique one, I mean the unique unique, unlike the other unique ones all, unique non-unique things and beings. Tallith. Tunic, which has no other, except life itself. The one that/she who will always have accompanied you. This is the mystery according to Jacques Derrida.

It's not that you love your tunic your unique tallith more than anything in the world, it's that there lives the only love that knows no substitution. And yet it has more than one secret, if not it wouldn't be faithful, your tunic, to your way of thinking nothing less. The analyst might ask about the overdetermining import-ance of the altogether peculiar traits of your own tallith, which will have earned it a kind of song of songs. For among all talliths and unlike them, your tallith is all white, like the beloved is white and like his beloved is black. The analyst might also wonder if there could exist another tallith all white and then slowly yellowed by time, if, let us say, 'something' were to happen to this your tallith, or if by chance 'my own shawl' this tallith, crossing the hymen of virginity could have a successor, or a twin, or a descendant, despite your desire to have done with inheritance.

I had therefore almost not touched this enveloped textual tallith. Put on guard. Thus will I not have read it well 'too late' as he had ordered, too late that is to say late, that is to say rather late. So that he might not accuse himself of having anguished the reading with the enormity of his anguish.

I have just reread twenty times page 35.

– No, because the point is that it is no longer me in question, precisely, but what we're here calling the verdict. A still unknown verdict for an indeterminable fault, all the perjuries in the world, blasphemies, profanations, sacrileges, there have been so many. In any case, as for me, I'm lost. But I'd still like it to happen to me [*que cela m'arrive*] and cause my downfall *thus* and not otherwise. Because I feel that the time of this verdict, if it could finally open up a new era, is so paradoxical, twisted, tortuous, against the rhythm, that it could mime the quasi-resurrection of the new year only by sealing forever the 'so late, too late,' in what will not even be a late conversion. 'A so late, too late, *sero*' (life will have been so short), a delay I am complaining about, feeling sorry for myself while complaining about it [*me plaignant moi-même en me plaignant de lui*]. Accusing, <u>*Klagen*</u>, *Anklagen*. But to whom do I make this complaint? Would it suffice to be able to reply to this question for the complaint immediately to have no further raison d'être? Is it to God? Was it even to Christ that my poor old incorrigible Augustine finally addressed his 'too late,' 'so late' when he was speaking to beauty, *sero te amavi, pulchritudo tam antiqua et tam nova . . .?* 'So late have I loved thee, beauty so ancient and so new,' or rather, because it is *already* late, 'late *will I* have loved thee . . .' A future perfect is wrapped up in the past, once 'late' means (as it always does, it's a tautology) 'so late' and 'too late.' There is no lateness in nature – neither in the thing itself, nor in the same in general. (*Veils*, 32–3)

How can one tolerate such a cruel beauty without complaining, without pitying oneself? Me neither, I do not know this when I write this sentence and pose this question. Who is complaining of whom to whom? Am I speaking of the beauty of the page or of that of Saint Augustine's God? Or of the mad beauty of the complaint?

Could one live without complaint or accusation or self-accusation, or hetero-accusation, that is to say without writing, without accusing oneself of living, of not living, no time, too late. 'I have just reread page 35' I noted this in a blue notebook 3 January 2004. I have just received your complaint sent in 1995.

But what kind of reading can one perform when one finds oneself to some degree invited, lodged, within the text to be read?

★

I will speak here as best I can about what comes to me, has come to me, three times already, from your direction, and differently each time, when I have 'found' myself in front of *Veils*, in front of *H.C. pour la vie*, and in front of *GGGG*, 'found' in front of even as I 'found' myself *within*. 'Find' is not exactly the word. I lost myself right away, as in my native city of Oran when as a child I had gone completely astray there, it was not me, it was not her, a great veil of fog enveloped us I recounted this in *Savoir*, which you, no sooner written, had 'lifted' from me (*piqué* was your word) so as to restitch it [*repiquer*] into your other veil-sail thus assuring it, by means of this transplanting, a sumptuous growth. Drawing my little text all the way toward your glorious chant (I can hyperbolize you shamelessly, I have always thought it. One day the little epic will have to be told of the several propitious contretemps in the journey of *Veils*.)

Where to put myself, *where* to begin – to read? For I am inside and outside. This is a familiar question. 'I don't even know where to put myself'[29] you said to the vast audience of psychoanalysts as you considered with elegance, exactness, perplexity, and humor the scene where, whether you liked it or not, consciously or unconsciously, you found yourself, for a time, put in the place of the Analyst of Analysis. And what you said on that occasion, I could almost apply it to myself.

> Without knowing – as regards the essential – without knowing anything, I advance. I have nothing simple or simply possible to tell you, and basically I know nothing. I don't even know how to admit that, to admit that not only do I know nothing, but I don't even know where to put myself, me and my nonknowledge, any more than I know what to do with my questions about knowledge and power, about the possible and the beyond of the possible. I don't know, to begin with, what, which title, or who authorizes me – certainly not myself. . . .
>
> And yet, you understand me very well, I have been authorized to address you, for the moment.[30]

With some differences in my case (1) with *Veils* I am not the analyst; I am (following)

– How do you know that? you will say to me

I understand what you mean – but all the same –

(2) The most mystifying thing here is the blow struck with *knowing* [savoir]

You, for your part, can say 'Without knowing – for the essential part – without knowing anything, I advance' (44; 256)

No one will contradict you. Wise is he who can say he advances without knowing anything for the essential part, philosophically analytically wise.

But as for me, in *Veils*, here I go 'advancing' while advancing without seeing before me a text called *Savoir*.

I should have called it, as a precaution, *Sans Savoir*. But it's too late. I will say in my defense that *savoir* begs to be pronounced with hesitation. From the reader's good graces

– Where to put myself? Where am I?

I find suddenly that I resemble somewhat that •, the black dot that floats between your stanzas in the manuscript – that I am going to designate now with the supertitle *Points de vue piqués sur l'autre voile* [Points of (No) View Pricked on/Picked up from the Other Veil] (these are perhaps the first words that came to this meditation. But one will never know)

This • would be altogether me: A point of (non-) view. I mean a point without sight, a pupil without light. • around which, from which, you execute your fascinating dance of Veils. But this • goes and disappears in the book *Veils*.

Where to place myself, now?

Where to place myself? is not the same complaint as *where am I* who am I that I heard you read you proffer more than once.

Where to place myself [*où me mettre*, where to go, where to hide] one says as one casts a look around for a crack a mousehole.

Where to go to be able to delight in peace therefore without 'me,' frankly, in the beauty of this text without accusing myself and pitying myself for too much and for too late?

★

I return to the manuscript.

Now you write: 'I know Hélène Cixous, note the present [you add 'improbable'] tense of this verb, for the last thirty years, and here since forever without knowing . . .' This is a now (from 1995) that is now ten years old. Hélène Cixous? So it is no longer a question of me, precisely.

H.C., at bottom, I have always doubted that I was she. When you call her, when you name her, I rise, I trust you, as for me I still have my doubts.

You, on your side, you know her with a perhaps, since a forever without knowing, and it's to me that you say:

– You know.

I give you my assent. What do I know? You, surely you know it.

This 'So it is no longer a question of me, precisely,' I've just lifted from you. It was a knot in a fringe from page 35. Neither to name nor not to name neither to sign nor not to sign. I already wrote that thirty years ago, forty years perhaps, at the setting of the Sun.[31] From *Portrait of the Sun.*

And now after the night, the day, you would say, where are we, where do we awaken, where do we keep watch on awakening this new us?

Buenos Ayres.   Le verdict
Écrit

vu de très loin, en par dans le coin le plus éloigné
ce soir, tout en bas d'une carte ; frôlé du dehors de Majella comme ti
lequel atteste le pointe de cette extrémité ; l'on accordait le nouveau
mettre, un heureux événement si ce soir plus ne révélera, une
vérité enfin si vrai que tout mais dit n'était une à voir avec un
dénouement — Comme si la vérité, si vraie y tout, attendait elle-même
une autre fin ; si l'écrit du voile ni disparition ni héroïsme, une
autre bien ne figurata, cher Odin, voilà pourquoi f l'autre mettre,
quelqu'un, pas sans doute (moi par exemple pourrait-on) vit
ne avait — ce serait la fin de l'histoire en ce sens. Fin de ti
fin de révélation — et sans   encore !

Chevaux de mort, histoire de voile —   Je connais le long ti sur,
notre ce présumé de ce verdict, depuis plus de haute aux, depuis
toujours sans savoir, sans que la main fin a faite confie
ici dans savoir , à savoir l'avant-dernière la vraie , faire
hypothèse , la révélation du fort — faire qu'il ne soit tout ce
seule hypo, un vérité presse avec elle voisine lieu
un sens à l'opération — la minute puis ante forte puis in
cette explosion pré-opératoire. Elle la voix déshervé ala ,
elle ne peut être dans la plus voyante facit la suite ;
pensée humaine, le prophète pas c'acque. Elle n'a l'écrit
par dit a ceux , qu'il soit . Ta en qu'il ne voir , ce n
forcé en déclos du fort n'a rien à voir avec la
révélation ou le dénouement , quelque voile de fin rédemption ,
quelque révélation . Et ce n'est pas faire de f savoir sans
savoir , plus fou ?   (1)

Trop d'évidence

En avoir assez, en savoir plus, [...] assez, de la vérité, [...] la poule
[...] tout, la vérité [...] hantise de [...]. Quel fatigue.
Mais "fatigue" ne veut encore rien dire dans [...]. Le mot
"fatigue" veut dire [...], demain, [...] faites [...]
[...] de la vérité [...]

C'est trop vieux pour moi, comme moi, la vérité.

[...] de tous les — de la vérité comme un vérité. Lassitude d'une
[...] et de la vérité, de [...]

(1) sans parler (inhabité) → cit [...]

(2)

Il a avoir aux (Salut (Saluts) d'écrire
de start-écrire

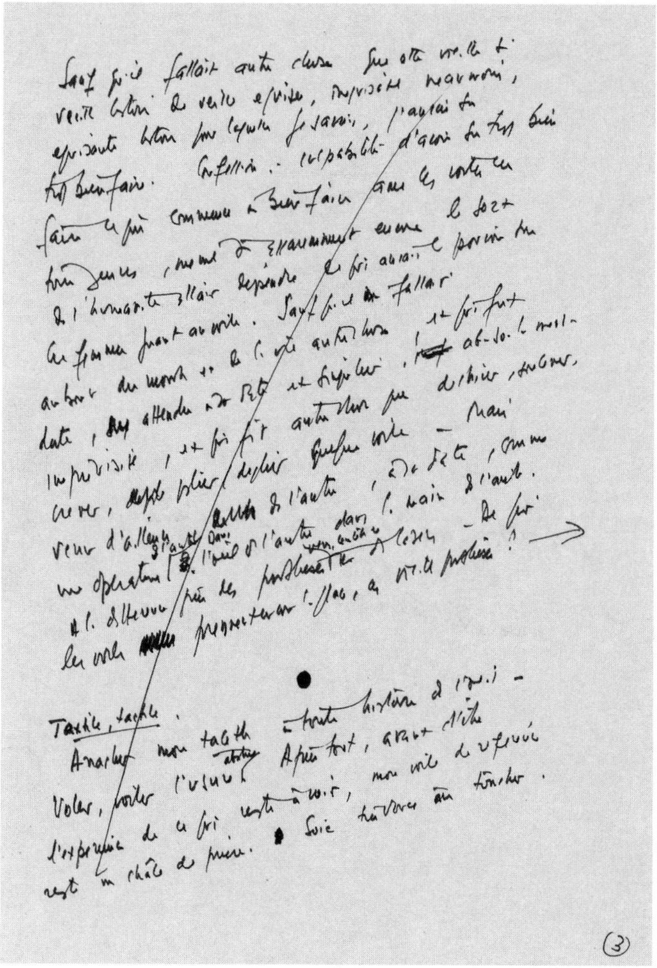

Bref. Il a avis aux (de luil, d la lu)
si traiter ou, si ti voir au on comm
l'aut. de laime lette.

Rien à voir avec [illegible] trois mots à carreaux, baisers, porter [illegible]

sur lui, parfois à même la peau. Il fut blanc d'abord.

vierge, le seul talith blanc de la famille, acheté à l'occasi[on] [illegible]

de mon grand-père maternel [illegible] Il devint un peu jaune [illegible] l'imprononçable [illegible]

maintenant. Je ne sais pas pourquoi mon père [illegible] je l'ai repris [illegible]

pendant quelques années. Après sa mort, [illegible]

[illegible] sans savoir [illegible]

Il faut savoir — au moins [illegible] aucun [illegible] talith — [illegible]

[illegible] la mort.

[illegible] la bénédiction [illegible]

le père [illegible] bénit ses fils — [illegible] les 2 [illegible]

de [illegible]

[illegible] un peu [illegible] dans le "[illegible]"

l'interminable [illegible] talith —

[illegible] enseveli [illegible] grand-père [illegible] blanc,

[illegible]

[illegible] les [illegible] blancs [illegible]

[illegible] talith [illegible]

[illegible] aurait [illegible] talith [illegible]

[illegible]

([illegible], Talin...)

4.

Relevons aussi le "problème de l'orthodoxie":
ta traductri, dans ta vente vivo suffit, l'vente, l'
vert la lui paroît d'un lang. d'art (? i m'as s'en lisons
sans voile traducta de tions. l'si doit écouter au peg...
Or. c'si bè ici' le mot la veut ??????
hai sulow ou mot du voi mais l'fami la
mot "voils (voile, la orl, voir, voie, voir, wre, verr...)
est traduisit en dehor de cef'on telle la france - en
proiber reid'art. ??? mot bent sons li ??? enrie
S'est langue ???? l' l'art ....

Mais un bète comun Sacri ??? la ???? ???
en Gavin. Il Divent d'lague, ??? la lus ???
??? de dir] on li er l'age ??? del r comun → n'est
senon wi er l'operta del ou, che ce
w un aut. (→)

(→)

tote au ??? cheque test J.H.C. ??? ??? na
n'a ??? ??? ?? li - en Gaven un Gaven. Reste à
venir -
   Annmer la tonder (test ???? - ??? ???
en angli + comun d tonke au (??? (un aton
extair.)
   ___

      la mette comme
      la mette comme verdiete
      (a verdieti

III

The Infinite Tastes of Dreams

'*Last night I dreamed of a guy who played at losing his time.* 'Don't waste our time.' *Someone says that. Very clearly in English. A message to be received in English.*'

(Dreamed by Jacques Derrida in 2001.)

From whom to whom? To whom does time belong? Who *has* time? 'Our time' is also our age, our epoch, our era, no?

★

'I ask myself why my argument with [*explication avec*] analysis in general and with psychoanalysis in particular has always had . . . the deathly taste of general delivery mail [*poste restante*], which has driven me to prowl endlessly . . . in the vicinity of *Beyond the Pleasure Principle*.'[32]

– Each one of your words, each segment of the body of your sentence, requires an explanation. An explanation is not exactly an '*explication avec,*' an idiomatic expression that harbors a shade of quarrelsomeness. Analysis, yes, we have always said this word, each of us,

123

rather than psychoanalysis, a way of situating ourselves near and against, right up against and against. One must imagine, therefore, another analysis. The one constituted by your whole philosophy. Your philanalysis.

What holds my attention is the taste of death in poste restante. What holds me in poste restante is the taste of death the dream taste of death

– In poste resisting. In post-resistance

– And also the endless prowling about [*rôderie*]. I see you prowling, lurking, loitering [*rôder*]. I also see you breaking in [*roder*], like a new car, making it run for the first time. I see you as a *rôdeur*, a prowler wandering beyond the pleasure principle. Thinking about pilfering, but like St Augustine, stealing some pears and grapes for the obscure pleasure of evil, not for the taste of the pears, or rather for the taste of their bad taste. I can hear you letting go a chuckle.

– I'm breaking analysis in. I'm breaking myself in to analysis. I make things turn, spin. I rascalize it endlessly. There is no end. There is no end to the taste of death in poste restante.

– The taste of death remains. Unfinished. Unfamished. The endless attracts you. As long as there is taste there is life.

– Life has a taste of death. The taste of death of life.

– That's what I was going to say. But you're the one who discovered it with the birth of your philosophy: the poison in the gift, and all those undeniable potions and mixtures the taste of which is pushed aside and denied by the majority of those who lack courage. You sensed right away this taste of finitude and that finitude has a taste. Me I didn't notice anything. It's moreover what differentiates us. You, it's as if you were remembering what is going to happen. You have it on your tongue. In your tongue. The very word *finitude* is unknown to me.

– Look, you see right here, I'm going home to Ris, I'm stuck, blocked.

– Blocked. There you are a *block*. 'A felled tree trunk.' A marvelous word. I give it to you.

– Millions of cars. When I'm stuck, blocked like this, it drives me mad. It calls up uncontrollable ideas of revolt in me

– Which you control

– My impatience in every domain

– Which you write in-patiently

– When I read, when I write, this is also what makes me cut across the field

– The hunted beast

– And the sovereign. Very close to the beast because it can suspend the law

– With that you could write a thousand different scenes. As with Poste Restante. You're brimming with things, with stings to write, with complaints: blocked, to posterester, to break in the unbearable taste of life.

– Have you ever been Poste Restante? No?

Not only have we mutually haunted each other, the poste restante and I, but it also draws supplementary strength when it rises up as a ghost in English. 'Dead letters' is what they call it.

– They are only a little more dead than the others. For Kafka all letters are destined for ghosts

– You, in *Manhattan*, you made me dizzy with all your fake true letters. Did I already write you?

In Manhattan there are crowds

The difference between you and me is that when you write, suddenly there are powerful singularities, Clarice, Beethoven. There is someone. Whereas with me, never.

– But with you there is someone and it's you

– Not in *Specters of Marx*.

– You think?

– Not in *Politics of Friendship*.

– Who says that the friend is the one who receives? That the absent ones are present? That the dead are living?

– Ghosts. But with you, who is Beethoven? I am looking for the transposition.

– A letter is always dead and from another angle eternally living

– That is what I mean. A taste of death remains as soon as there is posting. Everything arrives poste restante, remaindered. Everything arrives post, by the post, and posthumously. 'Why have I always dreamed of resistance?' (*Résistances*, p. 15). Why have I confided to you so often my regret at having missed what I would have liked not to miss at any price?

– Blowing up trains, tanks. The capture of German officers

– My phantasmatics are even a little suspect a little heroicophantasmatic.

– I've always noticed the *insistence* of this particular regret, so little in tune apparently with the other aspect of your childhood, equally insistent and confided, that of your fears, your fear of violence, of hostile types. It's as if you had been sent (by someone, them, the gods, and the destinies) into the wrong class, given the wrong advice. The urge to blow things up, throw bombs, cause the world to derail, you still have it.

– Unsatisfied. I've had enough of being unsatisfied.

– Resisting otherwise.

– Dreaming of resistance is the secret of my power. Of its powerlessness.

The taste of the Dream.
A taste of infinity. The infinite tastes of dreams. I live in the society of dreams. Like you in indecision. Like the subject in a sentence of Proust's, as if we were a bee gathering nectar from a basket of young girls. Our lips

heavy with dream upon waking. The infinite tastes of sugar

The Dream, *Le Rêve*. The desire of the dream has always preoccupied us. This character, this other text. This Visitor. Always so unforeseeable, unfordreamed. Bursting with secrets, infinitely desirable, a transformable *ver* [worm]. Amazing reversible *ver*. All our lives we talk about it, about the Dream-and-the-text, about dreaming, writing, not dreaming, the different lots that have fallen to us, he the intermittent dreamer, me impenitence itself, and there's nothing we can do about it.

That we have so often and for so long spoken of dreams, of dreaming, has to do perhaps with the original circumstances of our meeting. For it was as one haunted, urged on by dreams, hastened by the wind of the unconscious, troubled very young, too young to be maneuvering sailboats at night, too myopic as well to discern the end and the beginning of the dream as reality, reality turned into a nightmare, hostage of the excesses of literary, philosophical, oneiric texts piled one on the other that I spoke to him, addressing myself like obscurity to the light that I believed him to be or to have. He the masculine Sibyl. Naturally he answered me, oracularly. Literature, that's all I thought about, it was my dream. The dream always greater than any other world, more better and more worse, more creating, more genial. So ephemeral immortal. Vast giant born of a tiny creature of unknown chemistry. I was terrorized. He was welcoming.

It was wrapped up in the same shadowy shawl that I showed him – confided – my first debris, indefinable *scribbledehobble*, unnatured, excretions transexcretions of nocturnal visions, which I would never have called texts, aborted monsters, anguished descendants of their elder brother, my dead mongoloid son, species. As if I had told him one of those series of dreams each more trying than the other that I sometimes see arguing over my nighttime flesh. It was not the form that frightened me, for as they crystallized these spurts flowed into language, sculpted rhythms, discovered their manners, without my having to try very hard. It was the foreign and furious cause and states that these lavas projected, the in/can/descent indecency of the internal volcano that sickened my heart. In a certain instinctive way, I asked him for a *diagnosis* – what he would have called *a verdict*. I didn't ask for absolution. Nor a resolution. More like a localization: where was I wandering? On which side? Is this visionary eruption madness?

– Would I have wanted him to tell me yes? Or no?

He tells me: yes and no. According to him it is not a crime, but it is threatening all the same. But he can ward off the threat with words of praise, but, be careful . . . There is perhaps some good in the bad.

One could analyze endlessly the phantasmatic characters that we were then one for the other. We did not do that, it was coming.

★

Throughout life we tell each other our dreams right up to the end. We give each other these chapters 'to read,' for him unwritten for the most part, even though he has noted some of them, as for me they are all written. I mean: we say them, read them, cite them to each other, out loud. We show each other our lucky finds. We dangle our seashells, make them gleam like holy relics. These childish exchanges come in the wake or the place of Algeria: we pass each other our dreams like ageless epiphanies. We cannot dispense with them because they are so archi-originary, we don't even see it. Or else it's as if we were telling each other what we ate, what we wore. Insignificant things that make for a world. We used to say: *le Jardin d'Essais*. All of that is the Jardins d'Essais. Alchemists of the Verse-Worm

When I told you my Ant, there were without my saying it, thinking of saying it, naturally the ant colonies of Algeria. Insects: we were born with them. We don't need to say it to each other. We replay them for each other in the present. Between us, insects make words, words insect and insexion each other.

I would never have thought of talking about this, this traffic in reveries, and yet it was done. How can one not receive the dream by reason of reading? It is the stranger in the house, Elijah arriving always in the guise of the beggar who is necessarily welcome on Friday evening, his place set at the table by my grandmother or by his father, Aimé Derrida, in charge of hospitality for the community. It is unrecognizable Ulysses, unknown hero of the nostos of every man as not at home at home. It is incredible like Jacques Derrida. Literature begins twice: the first time with the Trojan War (war takes the name of the prey), the second time with the war around hearth and home. Displacement, substitution, error, blindness, secret secret. He's the one who began by spilling the beans, I say. He will say that it's not the one who begins who will have been the first to begin. He is more afraid and less afraid of the invaders than I am. He has always shown great kindness to my dreams. He could have preferred to chase them away or hunt them down. But he is gentle with wild species, with poets and beasts – at least with most of them most of the time.

It sometimes happens that a dream makes its way from out of the originary grotto to an unforeseen scene, as was the case with 'Fourmis.' It was in October 1990. The account Jacques Derrida gives of this voyage made by a dream – I am rereading it today, fifteen

131

years later – is in itself an exemplary masterpiece of the way Derrida has of bustling around a word, a molecule of the unconscious. Whoever observes the finer points of the movement will discover something like the invention of a brand new genre, an analytico-literary reading that is conducted philosophically starting from a living thing that is almost nothing (ant, word, insect, thing, very tiny) and reaches all the way to the most subtle depths of the questioning of the human being.

Conducted *in French*. By the thinker without equal, poetically well armed, and thereby the greatest.

I cite here a few lines in support of an ethical consideration:

> **Ant [*fourmi*]** is a brand new word for me. It comes to me from one of Hélène's dreams, a dream she dreamed and that she told me recently without knowing until this instant how this 'ant' would make its way in me, insinuating itself between experiences that resemble song as much as work, like the animals of the fable, one of Hélène's dreams that to my knowledge I am the only one to know, of which I will apparently say nothing, nothing direct, but of which I note already, because there was epiphany of an ant [*un fourmi*] in the dream, that it is very hard to see, if not to know, the sexual difference of an ant [*une fourmi*] . . .[33]

Each segment of this very long hypotaxis (which I interrupt here in the middle) obviously deserves meditation, critical analysis in every direction. Others will do that. To help me, I lift out merely these words: 'one of Hélène's dreams that to my knowledge I am the only one to know, of which I will apparently say nothing,' so as to borrow from them the necessary sign of caution and delicacy, marked in this sentence moreover by the repetition (calculated or not) of knowledge/ knowing: to my knowledge I am the only one to know. That is the sign of uncertainty, but sure of itself, that I take up for my own account and for everything that will follow in this chapter. We recount our dreams to each other. To your knowledge and to my knowledge, we address these accounts to each other. This does not mean that they will not have been recounted to others, recounted otherwise to others, and at other times. I tell you here that you were 'the only one to know' this ant, *ce fourmi*, then, absolutely alone, for I myself did not 'know' it.

But to whom does one 'recount' one's dreams? What does the word 'recount' tell us? To recount like an adventure, an event? To whom did I 'recount' and you to whom? (we, you and me, who are among those who do not recount ourselves to some professional analyst). To whom, in the morning, when the dream remains still in the house? To a person who does not

133

interrupt, does not crush the frail vapor, who tastes noiselessly, to almost no one. To oneself, near to oneself. To a self supplement. To the ear. To the ear that keeps watch.

One would like to go back into the cave or make it come back. One looks for the vent in the tent, the door, the keyhole not necessarily the keys. One wants to suck up the black milk again. One gives to be given back. One redreams it for oneself once again . . . and then adieu. One wants to suck once more on the taste of the dream *in the present*, make its memory return to *the self/itself*, pull the madeleine out of the blackout, rescue from death this little bit of me, that would mean possibility of the impossible immortality, to manage to save an instant is very grave, it is the most important of all nothings ('although I didn't know yet [*ne susse pas encore*], and had to [*dusse*] put off until much later learning why this memory made me so happy') sings the narrator of the cup of tea who sucks, that is, *suce* even though he does not know, *ne susse*.

Each recounted dream is a song of Gilgamesh on the path that leads to making death loosen its hold. It is a triumph of the present that maintains its exaltation for a long time, by force of evocation, immobile eternal for two pages above the jaws of nothingness. The jaws that I myself let drop in order to swallow up the grandiose little thing of joy.

134

The enemy of immortality is lodged within ourselves, between our teeth, our words, the weakness of our strength, the strength of our weakness. 'Each time it is the cowardice that makes us turn away from any difficult task, from any important work, [that] advised me to drop it, to drink my tea while thinking merely of today's little problems' (says the narrator, p. 46) –

and every other time a contrary summons advises us not to listen to the cowardly advice. As one knows from experience, no one can predict the outcome of this struggle, which is all in twists and reversals. As one knows very often one does not know if one wants what one wants. One wants. Without ever knowing what it means to want. Recounting wants – no one knows what. Not recounting wants – no one knows what. Perhaps the same thing along other paths.

You give, but what, the dream that is closed, still sleeping, still dreaming, the virgin dream, the flower, you give a thing that is full of mysteries, you don't know what they are, which is what makes for their great value, you return it to the envelope, the newborn of still-indeterminate sex. Semi-narcissism: I give it to you just as I do to me, a minimal trophy and a mark of trust that cannot be measured. Moment in the garden of innocence, of fear interrupted, of barely forbidden fruit. The innocence of my mother telling me, with a pleasure of a Proustian-aunt-who-insists-on-never-sleeping,

135

another one of those dreams qualified as idiotic, absurd, annoying, devoid of interest, ridiculous, without head or tail, that are not at all worth the trouble of being dreamed or recounted she says and that unbeknownst to her she is incited to share with me in a deliciously naïve way. Sinister dreams whose malevolent core I keep myself from interpreting.

The admirable childish innocence of the dreamer who, at 95 + years old, *cannot see* death approaching.

Your innocence at the heart of your prophetic account which you proffer while blind and deaf to the death you announce, taking advantage of deafness, deaf-mute that she is, absolutely amnesiac.

It's just barely that we've left our childhood behind at that age. Not to be able *to see oneself* see – which does not prevent thinking about it every day.

In any case, flower, fruit, or *fourmi*, one is happy with the gift even if it is poisoned. Doesn't it come from the beyond, proof, provided one has the force of belief or the philosophical might to propel thinking always a step further than the thinkable, that we are permitted – if we wish it (*mögen*) – to survive ourselves?

Often I recounted my dreams to him (it's up to me now to find a present, as he will always have done). Not all: that would have taken all our time. That would have taken him as analyst. We did not take ourselves to be analysts. And yet – there is always a little 'analysis' that flutters, discreet imponderable, in the air of these exchanges. A pollen. We recounted our dreams to each other, differently. In the same complicity, with very different affects. In the same innocence, with different blindnesses. 'As in a dream,' as we would say. With a curiosity for the signifier, a greediness for tastetexts, an inclination to jokes, *Witz*, witticisms, all those verbal penchants that lead us toward every kind of language activity or sport. With a curiosity for sighs and hesitations. And a curiosity for the abundantly stocked idiomatic storehouse of French, of which in any and every context we exchange a few specimens that the worms had not gotten into. For example, concerning his famous line 'dès qu'il est saisi par l'écriture le concept est cuit' ['as soon as it is seized by writing, the concept is cooked'], we spend a moment cooking up the whole array of cooking utensils, throwing in cook, woman, stewpot, oven and other variations apt to derail the recipe. And *Recets*! *Recet*, do you know it? Refuge, burial, catch one's breath. What a word.

I *recount* to him, I do not *show* him, I to not give him *to read*, to decipher these gasping accounts that are badly written just barely 'seared' still raw when they go into the oven of my drawer of dreams. From his side he *recounts* to me, as well. Sometimes it is a question of dreams kept safe apparently whole. Always very strong, stronger than he is, stronger than his structural movement of inhibition, of forgetting that he constantly remarks and regrets. He so loves dreams, he would so much like to retain them or perhaps precisely the opposite, we discuss both sides. If he retained them he would be retained, he would be surrounded, invaded, written, he would be led to literature which he passionately loves to speak about, to approach, that he likes to grab by the hair, by a lock, a thread, but in which he does not wish to stay except as the greatest philosopher who has ever camped out in this delirious hotel, an inhabitant free to leave. Your dreams, I say, provide the hidden force of your philosophy. Their might goes almost entirely into that astral forge. You forget save. Save when some dream suddenly raises its caravel over the site of every shipwreck. This is the case with the dream of the two Blind Men who are fighting with each other, which he mentions in *Memoirs of the Blind* by uttering it and withdrawing it so as to shelter it from a necessarily blind psychoanalytic reading.

And so on the night of July sixteenth of last year, without turning on the light, barely awake, still passive but careful not to chase away an interrupted dream, I felt around with a groping hand beside my bed for a pencil, then a notebook. Upon awakening, I deciphered this, among other things: '. . . duel of these blind men at each other's throats, one of the old men turning away in order to come after me, to take me to task – me, poor passerby that I am; he harasses me, blackmails me, then I fall with him to the ground, and he grabs me again with such agility that I end up suspecting him of seeing with at least one eye half open and staring, like a cyclops (one-eyed or squinting, I no longer know); he restrains me with one hold after another, and ends up using the weapon against which I am defenseless, a threat against my sons [*fils*] . . .'

I will offer no immediate interpretation of a dream so overdetermined by elders [*vieux*] and eyes [*yeux*], by all these duels. For many reasons. The idiomatic filiations of my dream are, for me, neither clear nor countable – far from it – and since I have neither the desire nor the space to expose here those that I might follow in a labyrinth, I will be content with naming a few of the paradigms, that is, a few of these commonplaces of our culture that often make us plunge headlong, by an excess of anticipation, into a misguided or seduced reading. This dream remains mine; it regards no one else. What I will say of it here by way of figure, a parable on a parable, will thus come from what I earlier called precipitation.

A dream from the year 1989 that will have been preceded and followed by several other dreams, overdetermined in this season – and which he confides in this immense book of clairvoyance – where for once he has

139

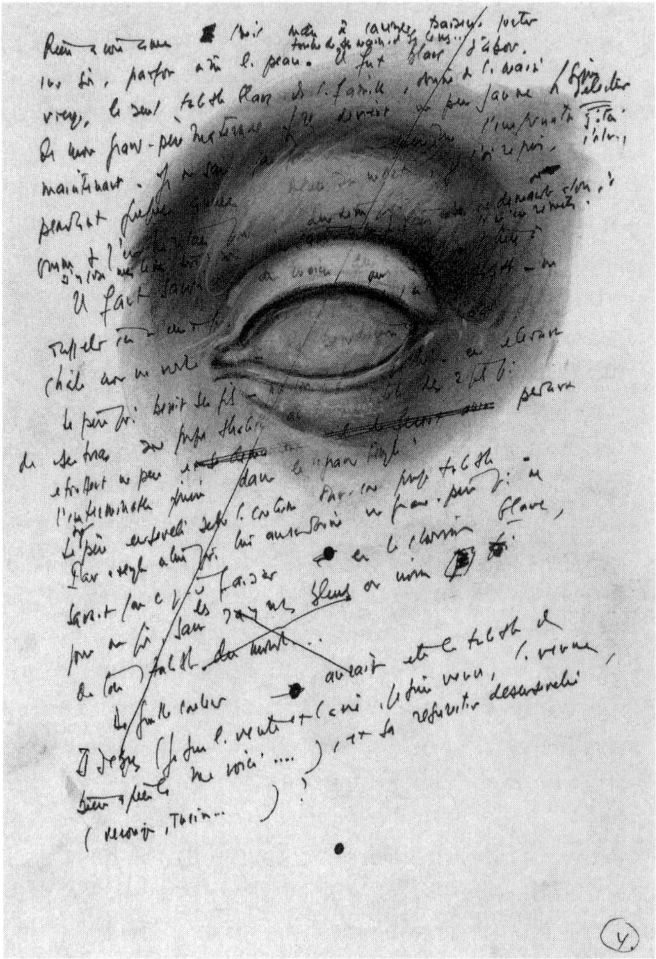

dealings with the *ophthalmologist* – A new *word* in the history of his body, but too present in mine – We come to an agreement around this time: if ophthalmologists are the blindest of the blind, with few exceptions – the blind are never blind. They are always seers. This dream that is given-withdrawn, there as if to remind the reader whose curiosity is awakened: this is neither a self-portrait, nor my self-portrait but, look at the sub-title: *The* self-portrait.

Look at me: I am winking my eye. Preterition? That's your affair.

– Ophthalmologists, you say, would be the blindest of the blind?

– Psychoanalysts, he says – are the greatest blind men.

– But the greatest blind man of all, he adds, the first and the last, is Jacques Derrida.

One has to see how he examines his dreams, first of all like a touching *blind old Isaac* – touching testing his Jacques, his younger one, recognizing *and* not recognizing him at the same time; then like a Jacob who in turn is blind, blessing in turn the younger one. In all of these tricks of blindness there is some hoax that is not bad.

Rebecca knows what she is doing when she causes her younger son to receive the blessing, says to himself Jacques Derrida the jealous younger son.

My mother, he says, I cannot know whether she sees or not. To what degree she sees or not. She does not look. He tells me about Esther Georgette Rebecca. One has the vague impression that she is directing her eyes. Her gaze stares at yours and you cannot say that she sees you. He tells me. And his account shimmers while performing the ellipsis of the subject.

At that time we are writing as usual each one on our side until the day we give it to each other to read. Often me first. Always between us the question of the 'who begins,' that is, who is going to be overtaken who is going to overtake, who is going to be duplicated who is going to duplicate, who is going to resemble. This time I begin, so he reads in *First Days of the Year*, *Self-portraits of a Blind Woman*. And it is as if we had dreamed the same dream with our eyes closed

When you read my little text where I mix memory and culture my stories/histories of the eye, you will be struck, he says to me, by what has happened to both of us. On the telephone we do not see the written figure of this story of eyes. Of more than one mourning. We dream of a same eye [*œil*], but our mournings [*deuils*] are different.

One has to dream and to dream well: to let dreams mislead us as to the subject, that's what Jacques Derrida suggests we think.

And what pleasure filled with wonder when one of these subtle creatures lingers near his side. 'This night,' he says, 'I dreamed of a place full of young Jews in kippas.' A seated Levinas does not recognize him. He leaves. Comes back. Levinas recognizes him and says: 'All these people who are asking me for answers that I don't have.' Levinas stands up, leaves. Instead of being short and fat he is tall and thin. I say: *Qui?* Who? *Qui n'est-il pas?* Who is he not? He says: 'Qui-pas?'

He says: 'This night I dreamed . . .' A little later I take notes, and while noting I notice the slight strangeness of the utterance: this night I dreamed. 'This night,' 'Cette nuit,' a very French expression – what is beautiful is the deictic, which replaces, doubles, a temporal indication by a spatial one. In English, you would say 'last night,' idiomatically. That's how language makes the world and history. 'This night' marks the date, there is (was) event.

The reader analyst will remark that I noted down Jacques Derrida's dream. I note quickly, early, I try – to be exact to the smallest detail. Just like for my own dreams, which are enormously different. We note each other.

One will ask oneself why. We too. We ask ourselves. For some reason we ask ourselves. Without asking ourselves. Mutually.

This doesn't go any further – at first. It can go further, no way to know. As it did with the dream of *Fourmis*. Or with those dreams that I'm recalling here, in the state in which they were told to me, without commentary. Dream, are you there? We are on the lookout. I take note the way I take note of the corners and folds of his texts. Of those of Proust as well. Or of Rousseau. The rich beings are books. Shakespeare's plays. Strange mirrors in which we contemplate ourselves in the other (in an) image. Everything becomes writing. Everything began in writing, by writing each other, listening to each other write to each other read each other.

The telephone is not for nothing in all this, as he points out with regard to the *d.s.* inasmuch as it is fabulous:

> There would be no speech, no word, no talking that would not say and would not be and would not institute or would not translate something like sexual difference, this fabulous sexual difference. And there would be no sexual difference that would not go through speech, thus through the word *fable*.
>
> This fable was given to me, like a word, by Hélène's telephoned dream. And as I asked a few minutes ago the question: 'What is it to give the word [*donner le mot*]?' or, 'What is it to give the thing?', 'What is it to give?', 'What

do we mean by "to give"?' before the word or the thing, I will advance the following thesis (in a dogmatic and elliptical fashion, so as not to speak a long time or all the time): if there is giving, it must give itself as a dream, as in a dream.[34]

Most often we 'gave' each other dreams as if in a dream, over the telephone. With the ear one sees better, that is, one dreams better, one has eyes only for the purloined letters. One has ties to God. One doesn't watch oneself as much, at a distance, one cares little about style, one makes believe, one can make oneself believe that one is addressing no one so to speak. A certain irresponsibility can be felt. You cannot see me. (I don't mean that you cannot bear to see me.) Thus I cannot see me, and this grants to each a freedom – that is conditional. This form of teleconfidence is suited to these still damp and groping accounts.

This does not prevent us from 'responding,' signaling, echoing. Each to the other, each invited into the other dream. From the beginning to the end, we listen to our dreams and play them back. Interpret? In the psychoanalytic sense? We never do that, at least not out loud, not so far as we know or say. Like translation, interpretation veils, he thinks. Any move to lift the veil is a movement that submits to the law of the veil. Likewise analysis winds around its navel.

It has happened once or twice, but no. As for me, I have explained myself a little in the 'Forewarnings' of *Dream I Tell You*.

It has happened that I hear, but I say nothing about it, I do not say that I hear, I hear too clearly that he is in the dream, that he is the one dreamed by the dream, that there is a powerful, amazing, vital necessary there

It happens, it has happened rarely and notably that he has some great, solemn, incredibly prophetic dream, I listen while shivering like one invited to the Mysteries and I say nothing. Warnings, premonitions, a whole blindfolded synagogue in which he cannot find himself.

It happens that a majestic and anguished dream grabs hold of him, 'poor passerby that I am,' he says, and drags him brutally in front of a high parental court. The violence of the event is such that he talks to me about it for a long time, in a restrained voice, that of a mythological prisoner, he has to answer for crimes he has not committed, he answers because he is accused, because he is accused by the dream he has to answer to it. And yet he didn't do anything he says in reality never at least nothing that he's aware of, in any case not really anything that deserves punishment if he had been able to do this bad thing he would not have done it if he had been able to dream this dream, he would not have done it, he has never *done* such a dream to his

146

knowledge as far as he recalls, he has always loved those he loves have always loved him, he could only have done the impossible and even so it would have been only in the thought of another in his dream he was only a passerby in this dream that put him in chains for no reason.

I note all this in my notebook for July 1995.

The dream is great like a Greek tragedy, inexorable and true like our crimes invented and hidden from ourselves by ourselves against ourselves, night overflows into day. There is no getting out of it. The voice of the pursued one rises feebly from the innermost depths of the interior *fort*, where fear confines it. That day I talk at length on the edge of anguish – I note all this in my blue veils/sails notebook – as if to clear another air in a jungle without waking. I talk, but I do not *say* anything.

As for him, he sends the ball back into my court. It is the end of September 2004. 'What gladness to see the preparations for a huge colloquium on you I say to him. What a crowd! One of your crowds. Obviously I'm not ready. I see all your admirers who take the plunge. All dressed. Me take the plunge? All dressed? I don't dare. Undressed neither. I can tell you moreover only a third of this dream. The apotheosis. There is an exhibition in a gallery. They are frescos of posters from colloquia. Fifty, a hundred maybe. This colloquium is the largest, it is the colloquium on colloquia, on all your colloquia. I see you arrive from the back of a vast hall, followed by the whole world, you advance through the whole room beneath the gaze of all those present, simple in triumph . . .'

Then you say: colloquoscopy. We laugh softly. This word throws a true, terribly true light on this triumph.

★

I am so grateful to the telephone, I say (we must be at the end of the last century, the telephone is growing and multiplying), I don't live without this cord, this *cordon*, I say.

– *Corps-don*, he says.

Yes, *corps-don*, *cor-don*. The descendant of the *oliphant*.

Thereupon we naturally do a spin on all the sacred horns [*cors*], among which the shofar. Not the *chauffard*, the hit-and-run driver. The shofar that resuscitates, he makes it resonate in *Rams*. One cannot hear sounded this remains of ram the shofar without feeling the shock of a fracture, in one's chest, of time. It is voice from the there, the voice that leaps out of the chasm, the opening of the lips of this world to that world after the end of the world. Nothing stranger and more mysterious than this interrupted animal cry, the human. It is as if each horn remembered having died for Isaac.

'This song of heartrending joy is inseparable', he says (*Rams*, p. 157), 'from the visible form that secures its passage: the strange spires, twists and turns, torsions or contortions of the horn's body,' he says, evoking in his language the tresses of the genres braided with those of the sexual differences in distress in which unfailingly all Jews recognize themselves and in which through their turns and the passages where their breaths expire recognize themselves as well all those who feel they are on the threshold of being abandoned by life, man or woman or beast in/spired by the announcement of mortality.

This *cor*, this *corps*, this *corne* call(s) and in the call recall(s). Recalls to itself, remembers. Brings itself back, alone, one on one with solitude, that of (the) being that calls itself on the telephone – knowing that None will respond in time, except for solitude. The call of No One.

It is not Isaac who cried out, suffered, to the sky. It is the ram, the condemned one without appeal.

'This song of heartrending joy,' you say. The horrible joy of the survivor, it is enough to rend one's own guilty throat.

– I imagine one day, he says, researchers, students will write theses on the telephone *chez* Cixous and *chez* Derrida, that is, in the texts, because there are many telephones in the texts, they are everywhere, everywhere, and thus I imagine when the telephone starts to become archaic, people will say: there, in the era of telephones those two wrote a lot on the telephone, he says this to me on the telephone, full of complaints, and complaints that have also been heard, but he will have said this to me more than once, said and forgotten so as to say it one more time for the first time. Another other time, said, written, published in *H. C. for Life* . . . for example. But each time is the first time. We are surprised by the telephone. Relieved, threatened, promised. He projects a past to come. I turn toward a past past, toward the dawn of the telephone, toward the premises and beginnings, the primitive telephones: birds flowerpots golden threads beginning with Tristan and Isolde and passing through Armance, the Princess of Clèves, the irascible divinities of Lost Time, how is one supposed to live cordlessly, without *cor*, without horn, without voice, we never stop describing and conjuring all the uncontrollable cut-offs of communication, figures of the ultimate cut-off, rehearsals and sketches, he always further out front in imagining imagelessly the teletechnological event, he always stands way off on the bow of time, searching the horizon, I am more likely at the stern, taking past misfortune as the measure of chances in the present.

His way of turning round, blind, toward the unanticipatable. His way of imagining a retrospective future.

As if his waking, his vigilance, vain telescopy he calls it, placed him there, the perfectly clairvoyant lookout for the danger that will not fail to strike without warning and where it is not expected.

Two very different attitudes in the face of destiny. And that is why, this is one of my hypotheses, we are attuned like two complementary gazes, posted at the two extreme points of time.

Him – expecting the to-come. Me – waiting for the Comebacks, the *Revenirs* – And thus expecting Revenants.

To come back to Dreams [*revenir aux Rêves*] and thereby to come to or return to *H.C. for Life* . . . the book in which he exhibits for the first time in public the 'theorem-of-the-two-sides,' thoroughly, confidentially, philosophico-analytically –

– to summarize, according to him H.C. is for life on her side J.D. on his side is on the other side, that is to say on his/her side, *de son côté* – for one understands as soon as one writes on this subject *in French* that it is not so easy to polish off the possessive pronoun *son* – but this is only an extremely tiny allusion to an immense theme – one of my hypotheses, regarding this difference – that he expresses underscores signs for his part and for which he is the apologist and the champion without my countersigning, a fragile hypothesis but one that can prompt reflection, is that we are him and me subjects and results of primitive scenes that are very powerfully different and influential – one could say overdetermining, of those 'first sorrows' (says Kafka), first mutilations, first biting pangs of death, which come about during childhood and whose unconscious tracings in memory mark us or wound us in a chiasmus. I see us, children, in a similar and fearsome context (colonial, Vichyist, racist, anti-Semitic Algeria) first of all stigmatized and expelled by a same decree (the anti-Jewish laws), similarly banned (with to be sure numerous traits and variations that we have described more than once each of us from our side). And on top of that attacked by death, but here very differently. Him, at age ten, witness to the death of the younger brother, a sensitive, receptive, thoughtful witness. Me, at age ten, put outside of life by the death of my father, deprived of world, god, roof, strength, skin, self

Two experiences that cannot be superimposed. On his side his dead brother, not him. In me my father dies and does not die. In each me some notme falls and gets back up otherwise. The brother a you who is more or less me than me. The father a more than me for me. He's hit in his fellow likeness, me I'm decapitated. Around the events, details confided by one to the other, which I will not report here. We were always careful not to open ourselves up to 'authorized' 'analysis.' That does not prevent feeling at a touch the furrows of the scars. Nor putting forward readings at an improbable rate. I tell him that at ten years old I lived *in reality* what he writes in phantasm with a 'flagrant truth' so many times, and that is gathered up in Celan's line '*Die Welt ist fort, ich muß dich tragen,* ' which he has literally *made his* through the force of love and imagination in *Rams*.

'Imagination' is what? It is *asif*. As if already in advance he had *in reality* lost the world. Like all of you, I am always dealing with this *Asif*. It is his, absolutely. It is an asif that holds 'reality' so tight, rubs against it, hugs it, asifpenetrates it, one can no longer discern the dividing line, it has an hallucinatory, hallasifinated force. I lived that, I say, and I wrote it, I *had to* write it, that is the *muß*, in order to survive my death, right away, the next day and then each time, so often, that the ground of the world was withdrawn at one blow from beneath my feet, I had to weave a ground from paper on which to set down *ich* and *dich* I've never done anything else. To the displeasure of my mother who despairs for me over what saves me but for her is only a burial. She does not call that living, she is no doubt right, but it is all that remains to me.

Him, it is as if the bomb fell exactly in the spot where he was standing a second before. He dreams often of bombs, bombardments, particularly in honorific vicinities. Marguerite must have felt the shock wave dozens of times. A 'that could have happened to me,' 'why not me' thus 'why me' won't leave him alone. I am not forgetting the brother before just before him, whose death precedes his birth just barely. Save, him. One knows it

the Save, the *Sauf* haunts him. (*Sauf:* what a word, with its countless resources, anagram palindrome.) The one who is still living, who just escaped. He could have 'leaped' [*'sauter'*]. He leaps otherwise, a sidewise leap. Save to the side. He lives under imminence. In Reality-under-imminence. He lives like a safe-by-mistake, a fake safe [*un faux sauf*], a debtor who is going to have to pay in a little while. Time hurries him.

I am not forgetting that one scene always refers back to another scene, before this scene, another scene, I am not forgetting the referralship [*renvoyage*] of decon-struction, the counter-genealogical movement of deconstruction, the trace is an irreducible liaison, he recalls this with more-than-pedagogical insistence,[35] he has had enough, for himself first of all, for me and thus for you, of the phantasm of once more seizing upon the originary. I am not forgetting that each time I call him, designate him, paradigmatically by this name of Derrida, I make as if I knew whom I was talking about or what whereas not at all, I know so little, and in the instant there is one of them, another one, there are so many ones in him that are dissembled beginning with resemblances that are ephemeral but vivid but tenuous, and each one uniquely him. 'You know me a little' he says

– Oh, that a little! Another impossiblittle!

He is 'full' of spares, Hamlet (two at least by that name), Socrates by the dozens, Abrahamisaac-and-the-ass, in turn and each turn very brief, very full, evanescent. There are traces, all referralshipped. The time of all times hurries him.

(Almost always fathers with sons, fathers that have sons, fathers filled with the complaint of the son, referred back to the son. He pities the child. He pities the one that he is[36])

The note of the 'why me?' resonates as soon as he autobiographizes a little. It is the astonished sigh of the elected one. The elected one that he is for-better-and-for-worse. The best and the worst inseparably. Set-apart one knows not why. For the only white tallith in the family. Tallith to be endlessly read. 'It was given to me by (the father of) my mother, Moses. Like a sign of election, but why? Why me?' (*Veils*, p. 44). Just as he reads the tallith the tallith reads him, binds him [*le lit, le lie*]. The elected one elects himself, say I to Elijah. For he knows how to read. He knows that everything is to be read. That is, interrogated. But without ever counting on a response. He would like to know

Whyme, knowing full well that I do not know who me is, who is me.

So then, dreams? Scenes of whome par excellence.

I have my rendez-vous. I expect my revenants there. With impatience on my side, patience on the other side.

As for him, he has so admirably described (in parentheses in *H. C. for Life* . . . p. 69:

(Let me say in parenthesis, once again since it is agreed that I shall not be speaking of myself, I believe my eyes all the less, in front of this miracle, since I, who am still on the other side, run on the contrary on the dream's interruption, more or less, and I write when *my* awakening, unlike her own awakenings, I suppose, when my first awaking begins by turning off the current of the phantasm and putting an end to the night. The phantasm can then cut a path through what I write only unbeknownst to myself, without my authorization: I betray my dreams, in the double sense of the word 'betray,' I abandon them I leave them and let them come back only in the guise and disguise of symptoms which in turn betray, belie and deny me. I am therefore in betrayal in all respects. I live and write (on) it. She does not; another element, another way, she has the power and the grace to authorize her dreams. Therefore her dreams, because she remains faithful to them, are consecrated, enfranchised and ready to enter writing, to be admitted into the holy orders of writing, *authorized* as author's dreams, as one says author's privilege, author's signature, author's copyright, author's correction. To be on the other side, for me, means being at once less conscious and less unconscious than her. Therefore less fast as well. I close the parenthesis.)

on the one hand on the pretext of not speaking of himself in this book, save, save in parentheses, and as if this book were not speaking of him from one end to the other, since it is he who reads her, me who reads him, and on the other hand because when it is a question of his dreams, he parenthesizes them by definition) how he *betrays* his dreams with two inverse-and-simultaneous betrayings, the one by abandoning them, the other by giving them thereby the chance and the power to come to betray him disguised, once they've been forsaken, as symptoms, thus to make him say unwittingly what he does not want to say, otherwise said what he wants to otherwisesay without saying it, for he loves only the otherwise [*l'autrement*], the otherlies, the one that lies without lying. To be sure we are moved, led to dream in apparently opposite ways. If I write on dreams, as he says, that is, *au rêve*, the way one says '*à la voile*,' on the force of or powered by – I write also *au rêve*, that is, to the dream, I never fail to do so, I have an invisible

157

altar on which every night I leave a request. I pray the dream to come. What is more I make detailed requests that are not taken into account. I want to be visited by my beloved dead. I am used to being disappointed. I make myself be infinitely patient. Whereupon, without warning, without apparent cause, one nighttime day or another my revenants answer my prayers, generally, I am used to this, when I am close to discouragement. But the reverse also happens: they come often of a sudden, for a long time, experiences of grace. That is why I spend half of my time 'on the other side' in another kind of life.

As for him, why would he linger like me?

Obviously none of this can be ordered up. To each one a fate is attributed. I mean the fate at the end of a struggle between all the forces that we align some for and against the others in our inner forum for against ourselves.

'I run on the contrary on the dream's interruption, more or less,' he says. He says 'I run' or 'I work,' *je marche* is his word. I say: the interruption of the dream makes you run or work. He says: *tu me fais marcher*. With these words, interruption of the dialogue. How will 'tu me fais marcher' be translated? (You make me work, you make my wheels turn, you lead me by the nose, you're pulling my leg, you're taking me for a ride, you're leading me up a garden path). And what precedes?

He writes by day, when it is daylight. He is the one who makes it, the day, the daylight. He *makes* the day. He is not it.

What he confides in me about these dreams is contradictory, a mixture. Analytic according to his always informed refined approach, for he is the greatest reader of Freud I have ever encountered. He hears everything Freud says, with passion, friendship, extreme precision, in German and once the straits and detours of thought have been crossed he allows himself to carry it with delicacy beyond itself, as if he were delivering it of its finitude, as if to analysis had come a Freuderridian time. A superfidelity freed from the obligations of inheritance.

He has a great nostalgia for his dreams. Those that flee him, obeying an injunction of the interrupter that he is willingly-unwillingly, leaving him at the same time in the lurch. Desires from above desires from below, inextricated. '*Son compte est bon,*' he thinks, that is, literally, his or her calculation or reckoning is correct, but idiomatically it says: he or she or it has had it, is done for. One doesn't know to whom the pronoun refers. He senses that there is something good for him in these confiscations, but there is another who doesn't give them up without regret. From this tug-of-war he recognizes that he is at the head of two camps. When dreams make themselves scarce, they are, one guesses, more highly valued. His economy is on the side of the small quantity, a little bit that can do much more than a lot. You should see his pleasure and his excitement when by chance one of them washes up on shore, still living mammal that he hastens to take in, miniature whale who brings him news from a withheld sea.

Elsewhere he knows a great deal about it, about what he calls aporias, about paralyzes and paralyze, about the knots that one gets oneself tied into, and about the fact that there is *some* meaning and *some* truth (quantities therefore) in the resistances that oppose their forces to other forces. 'The Penelopian or counter-Penelopian task of the *Deutung*,' he says, 'which is, after all, an analysis . . . it is a knot, threads to be untied, and *untied where there has been a cut*.'[37] It is thus a matter, for him, not of being a Penelope counterpenelope but of *thinking how* the cut can tie a link or *how the liaison* can be *the interruption itself*. That's what mobilizes all his forces, all his intellectual libido and all his experience of suffering: not the taste for interpretation, but the necessity of making thought pass through strictures that squeeze the breath out. To make thinking think, in the tightest quarters with itself.

It is not easy to get everyone to *swallow* this, this slipping through a strangulation. He begins over again all the time each time otherwise. He does not want to put an end to it by cutting. The interruption, a *'certain interruption'* of a *certain dialogue* can 'become the condition of comprehension and understanding,' he writes in *Rams* (p. 21).

'*I called* then . . . *to* a certain interruption.' *To call to* the interruption, to keep the desired one alive.

I recall that he himself *runs or works on the interruption of the dream.* Notice he says *interruption* and not *forgetting* of the dream.

It would be necessary to reread the immense reading conducted in *Resistances* of the subchapter on 'The Forgetting of Dreams' at the beginning of Chapter 7 in the *Traumdeutung,* where *Everything is Said* about those tangles that form knots in our throats and that lead him to dream about not answering, for the dream, to dream about dreaming without answering for the dreamed, for the dreamer, while talking, dreaming, without saying anything, neither the yes nor the no, to dream of *there where everything* is said without confession without infringing upon the secret the *there where* of literature.

'There where': the very place of resistance.'[38] Where is Therewhere? *There.* Or *where.* In literasure.

What is he doing with Freud? He rubs shoulders with him, he meddles and fiddles with him. He Freuds with him. Joyce would say that he Frauds with him. He is taken with him. Freud, now there is his other. A noble adversary who resists him enough for his victory not to be easy, thus for him to take pleasure. He likes to read what resists him well. He becomes Herculean with Freud. For each round, and there have been many over the years going back a long time, he pushes further beyond the beyond. He becomes superherculean. The tunic burns him, he is burning to analyze it. After all, Freud, psychoanalysis, is concerned with what haunts him, it is through analysis that he is best out of tune with himself. One day people will study Derridanalysis.

★

To come back to dreams. (I notice that I am deferring or drifting, just as when I want to approach the heart or the navel of a fiction, right away it centrifuges, just as when working on the seminar he calls 'The Beast and the Sovereign,' he wants to get to the Wolf and to the Lamb, but there they go fleeing from week to week, or else he is the one who flees, it is he whom he flees, he the wolf and the lamb.)

What he is able to do, the work, the monumental reading, with the other dream, or the dream of another. For example with Fourmi. Or with Fichu. How he multiplies them, pluralizes them, makes them teem like anthills, flutter and fall, sets them ablaze with meaning. As if he were himself the dreamer and the analyst that he is not properly speaking, but is otherwise. He takes his share, partakes. I observe him. He places himself at the intersection of me and you. At the crossroads. There where it touches him. Where he sympathizes. Where passion passes, the painful affect that makes being animated. There where he hurts in the other. As he will have confided to us about hurting in his mother in 'Circonfession.' To hurt in the other in oneself is not to send the hurt into the other, it is to receive into oneself the other's pain. The other's anguish comes to him, happens to him. It is not an appropriation. It is a co-sensibility. An impossibility of deciding between whome and whoyou. Sympathy. Compassion. A 'hospitaliarity' of the imagination.

A hospitaliar refinement, a nervousness for others who rarely meet. On the telephone, I say to him: 'My mother just fell flat!' 'Ow!' he exclaims. Not: ow! ow! ow! But: Ow! As if he were himself his mother, my mother, the mother — himself who fell flat. I was frightened. But all is well. One day I will have to describe this particular kind of high-intensity animal imagination.

The Tealephone Ceremony

I telephone him a dream. Not given therefore, therefore not taken back.

Tendered over the tealephone. It seemed to me good that it was good, refreshing perhaps. Simple ceremony.

Just as with the Proustian cup of tea, there emerged from it flowers, garden, oven, bakery, the nights and days of sexual differences, a whole natural history museum, the legend of centuries and sciences, Shakespeare, conjurations, separations that hormonize amorous colonies of insects and other peoples, the memories of all the Greek, Christian cultures, mythologies, treasuries of literatures.

History of a miraculous procreation. There has been gift. Indisputably. As he says to me with a smile,

(. . . Hélène furnished me *unknowingly* with the word *fourmi*, giving it to me thus. Her dream gave it to me without knowing what it was doing, without knowing what I would do with it, without knowing period, because one can only give without knowing. Her dream gave me the word not only as a term that I would play on today without playing, but as a word, and no doubt a thing, a living winged being, that I had never before seen in my life. It is an epiphany in my language and in the world that is tuned to it. It is as if, blind, I had never seen '*fourmi*' before, neither '*fourmi*' the noun, nor '*fourmi*' the phrase nor *fourmi* the thing or the animal with or without wings, and even less the *fourmi*, someone named *fourmi*. My God, who is it? Who could be named *fourmi*? And how he's changed!)[39]

– *Un fourmi bien fourni*, a well-equipped ant. I fourmish you with the word of the dream.

– 'Her dream gave it to me with knowing what it was doing, without knowing what I would do with it, without knowing period, because one can only give without knowing.'

It is true that my dream doesn't know what it is doing. It gives itself. Without calculating. But all the same. Not to just anyone. But fearlessly. Unreservedly. I telephone my dreams that do not know what they are doing only to the blind giver who knows what knowing without knowing and without seeing means. I am not as blind as all that.

Now the dream is his. It is his dream, his *fourmi*, his *fichu*. He is the one who gives to be read. Gift is altogether in Reception, Interreception, Interrupception. He does with it as he likes. No interpretation. But a hymn. Hymenoptera to literature.

★

J.D. dreaming

Notebook 1995

He recounts to me: three dreams. Three bits [bouts] *of dreams he says*

Three bits of dreams. One: my father was dead and in his coffin. I was supposed to go with others to take it/him by the handles to transport the coffin. At the moment I approached the coffin on the side on the lateral edge a dog's head comes out, a long neck like a whole dog, immense, with at the end [au bout] *a black dog. Hence enormous difficulty taking hold of the thing. It is so monstrous.*

And the same *night I dream: It's a young boy, being hunted pursued, guilty, who had some problems with the police, was going to be arrested, and who as a kind of arrogant provocation steps up to the edge of a café and with his hands full of appetizing things for animals, fish, meat, and he throws* it, there where I knew the beasts were going throw themselves upon it and eat. An amazing image: twenty or so dogs mad with hunger, rabid, who tear each other apart, who flay each other and the young man did it for that, to provoke a kind of animal cruelty, of war to the death among the animals, in order to grab what he had thrown them to eat. Strange huh? That's all I recall. Dogs in both of them.

You spoke to me about Tobit's dog [who I put into Messie]. That day Derek Attridge gives a lecture on Coetzee's revenant dog. I allowed myself to talk about Tobit's dog. I said a word about it, huh: [He laughs] A piece of your dog

Third dream this night – of another sort: I am in charge of an enormous airplane, a Boeing – and I must take care of this airplane, I move it I manage to put it in the corner of the city I park it. Chirac seems rather satisfied. After I must always calculate the flight/theft [vol] of this airplane, as if from a control tower, dashboard: the whole world

22 August 97 a large dog was biting my hand I was driving a vehicle, for a long time my hand was in his mouth, a big, enormous wolf-dog. What do I do? It was very painful. I had my hand in his mouth, he didn't want to let go. A big dog. I could have put pressure and hurt him. He had a wounded paw as well.

Saturday 30 August 97
How I dreamed this night! It was Lacan who was talking showing off, displaying large teeth spectacularly large and

beautiful that were not his. I say this in the direction of my predecessor, one mustn't take curaçao, cure à chaos – coffee – chaos – can make you sleep. – May one pose an objection? Is it necessary to be ill for coffee to have this paradoxical effect? He is very embarrassed.

Dream J.D. May 2002
I had a dream. My father played the saxophone very well. After him I tried myself. Not the least sound. I didn't even understand how it was possible. While telling you this, I associated with the shofar. It's difficult to blow into a reckless driver, that is, chauffard, *this horn*
My uncle was blowing/whispering a message: longs, shorts, breves, images of power.

★

That May I had no voice. He says to me: Stay on the right (voice)track.

IV

It's My Fault

(I am listening to him) –'Are you listening to me?' –
'Yes of course.' I said he pays close attention to what I
say. He listens, watches, records, sends back 'what I say,'
and that is what I mean. I am speaking here of reading
what is said. This scene is so old and so familiar that it
does not stand out against a background; it blends into
our perpetual confab. He pays extremely close attention to what I say in my language, and even more to
what my tongue says, since my tongue speaks his
tongue. I believe I am able tobeabletosay that a large
part of this attention, which is finicky – yes it is, yes it
is – is overdetermined by the fact, which precedes us,
of this common good: we speak to each other in the
same language, language itself, the one he loves but to
which he cannot surrender, the-one language, the
one that makes him monolingual, his Element as he
affirms. Whereas for me, German the other language
will have protected me from the one. He is attached to
French as he is to melancholia. A certain French *in
which* he breathes, aspires to live, to remain, everything

happens to him. In this natural supernatural French, the cause of his passions, we found ourselves/each other without being able to explain how, without being able to do anything about, we suddenly met inside its milieu without having seen ourselves enter, already cultivating it like the Jardins d'Essais in Algiers where we still today continue to take walks. He is the guardian of the Jardin d'Essais. When he finds me there he calls it the 'Jardin des C.' (see *H.C. for Life*), he supervises my goings. It is this language, our uninheritance, that commanded this first alliance, on whose basis we together practice separately heresy. He declares this language, this *franC*, at the borders, between the public and the private, as a having that is not his. No one can imagine a worse torment of thought. He is with it/she is not with him. He puts on an amazing scene with it/her, and makes a work without equal at once finite and nonfinite. And thereupon, master and slave of his slave mistress, jealous like a mortal, like a Moor, he desdemonizes her, he would kill her, he adores her. He will have addressed His Hymn to her, to his language. No more admirable celebration than *The Monolingualism of the Other*. No one has ever seen the like, a more ardent more raging, more loving self-portrait. He looks there like no one else. Well, this language that puts him beside and outside himself in it, that holds him outside it inside it, that possesses and dispossesses him, that loses him in its pocket that he swears is not his, it is as if this French were his virgin his daughter his mother his lover his two sons he keeps watch over – what? the purity? the honor? – like a jealous man. She/It is not his but still better worse he has no other he claims (the fact that he loves, trains, gallops more than just one other with an admirable expertise in no way diminishes his phantasmatic sworn faith: there is only one that is the One). He has not even lost it

He takes care of it like a purebred, male or female, he mounts it, fawns on it, flatters it, cares, combs, braids its hair, its mane, it straddles him or else he does. He cannot bear that anyone fiddles with or forks his tongue, that anyone filches it. Or borrows it from him

Moreover he never stops inventing it: thus, no one before or after him

And yet he's happy if someone steals it from him a little but in the neighboring field otherwise it would not exist to be desired. He does not deny that I am from the Jardin d'Essais. It also happens, when he is 'tired, tired,' that he says to me: you go ahead, then I'll apply the spurs. But if I scratched it, this language, he would have my hide.

I say that he listens to what I say and first of all *how* I say, he has trained ears that keep strict watch that I say correctly, handsomely, it has always been and it is always like this each time and from the outset, spontaneously. I keep watch over myself as well, a little, a little alert lights up, very little but all the same, as soon as I address him as soon as I sense we are speaking language to each other, then it's as if we were playing a certain native music, for two voices, with intervals, two voices, each haunted, especially his by a chorus that is often tense and conflictual, I keep an ear's eye on myself. We talk to each other at a run, with rapidity, anxiety, jubilation, like fugitives, we are of the same flight in truth. Since forever I listen to him with head raised, my ear's eyes never stray from the somewhat somnambulistic funambulist that he is, knowing very well that at every step he is running more than one language. Not only do I endeavor to allisten to him, but also in good faith, I want to listen to him, yes, I make it my task to listen to him, in other words to obey his path markers. More than one listening in an I listen. And how to listen to him well and thereupon listen to him when he equivocates and acrobats in his other French? I do whatever it takes.

Except for the mistake.

There is a mistake. There is only one, and it is mine. I don't know how, why, whence it comes, I make it, or rather it causes itself to be made by me, I am its committed servant, I don't see it coming, moreover if he wasn't there to blow the whistle on it, stop it stop me, land the blow, stomp his foot, clap his hands, catch me, shout: 'Again! There it is! You did it again!' I wouldn't know anything about it.

He never lets it pass

It is serious? Yes, it is serious. It is a French grammar mistake, *une faute de français*. He shouts, I start in horror, I could flop on a hairy back and wave my little monstrous paws in front of my nose. I'm screwed, skewed, undoed. It's as if I had it on my lips, I can tell from his irritated look.

And naturally repetition compulsion

A real mistake, a true fault, therefore.

And he, once again, *derechef*. ('Derechef' is for him: I give him this word to suck on, he'll like it.)

– How can you do that, you? I will denounce you, he says. – Correct yourself, he says –

– *Ich möchte so gern*

I would like to, I would so like to. But it does not give in. It, *elle*, she, she who? It/She? Or me? She/It comes back.

Every three months. Every three me's.

What to do? The One of us is stronger than the other

It would seem that she builds up strength when and when she is repeated. I cannot say that I do it or that I do not do it.

I want not to do it, or at least I would like. Don't I want to listen to you? I am sure that I would surely not want to stand up to you.

I am going to reread *Resistances*.

This mistake demands an explanation.

I never make it in writing. That too demands an explanation. It's not that I chase it off the paper. There must be something in the voice, in the other voice, in interlocution, a slope a hole, right away it slips by, it gets ahead of me. Or rather she does. There she is. It's a disgrace. You will never tire chasing after her. In 2004 alone you report me four times, if I remember right. The last time, in September 2004. Again! I'm a pitiful sight, I recriminate with myself, I don't understand myself, I panic. I moan:

— *Je ne sais pas qu'est-ce que je peux faire!*

— And there you go again!

Alas! There she is again! There! There! Just above. Three lines ago.[40] He becomes indignant. *Qu'est-ce que!*

— *You*, how can you — *qu'est-ce-qu*ate?

— How can you ask me that, *you*?

I grab for the cauldron: it's not my fault!

(1) *I can*not do it. (2) I thus do the impossible. (3) If I do the impossible, it can only be for you. (4) As for me, I do nothing. It undoes itself through me in spite of me. (5) All of this is to please you

I swear that I will do everything I can do to undo myself of it

Me too I wonder how I can make this mistake. Perhaps it's not my mistake, not my fault. It's not a mistake of my mother's. And what if it were a *pied-noir* mistake? And if it was not me but my brother? I question him. According to him, no, it's not his. It is my fault, my mistake, without any doubt.

I call my daughter, the grammarian *par excellence*

– A mistake?

No, she's never noticed anything

It's thus his mistake, it's his. I mean the one that is destined to him, to Jacques Derrida.

– It's for you that I don't do it on purpose I say.

Will I ever see the end of it? How will I know it? At the end of how much time without mistake may one think of oneself as cured? Absolved. Whitewashed like snow

Have I not always faulted in his honor? For his advantage? Or for my advantage? No, no. What benefit? It doesn't even make me laugh. It would not be impossible. But you are so scandalized. I would like to be a mouse. And for there to be a hole. But I am merely *Ungeheuer*

– It's the only reproach you'll ever hear from me in my life, he says.

Ha! Here's a clue perhaps: he's indeed counting on having always something to reproach me for.

A stain on the tongue!

– And you, you don't ever make a mistake?

Here I ask him an indiscreet question, with caution, timidity, courtesy, curiosity, and the obscure fear of accusing him. Me, I have never caught him out in a mistake, never a French mistake, no mistake or fault dedicated to me, not the least weakness, no fault for which I could reproach myself congratulate myself as the cause. But who knows if by chance, in my absence? Not that I want to make him ever confess

– Never. I never make a mistake.

His voice is clear, sure. Without the least doubt.

– I notice that, as for *me*, he says, I have kept a number of superego tricks from my school days.

I am thus alone with my fault (and his reproach)

How not to go on deserving his reproach?

Postscript
From Life

(While waiting for the veiled verdict Boulevard Raspail 1995)

– *When I first knew you you were still Bordelaise*
   – *I am from Montaigne. I am in Montaigne. Every year I essay again. I am going to make a tour, a tower of Montaigne*
   – *This afternoon I feel like taking up Montaigne again*
   – *Taking him up again?*
   – *Are you taking issue with me again?*
   – *I'm making it over to you. I make over Montaigne to you as well.*
   – *Two French semi-Jews*
   We the two French, Judeo-marrano halfJews.
   – *The alliance with the signifiers, where does that come from?*
   – *It comes from the alloy. The mixture* [mélange].

179

– *You're mixing things?*

– *I'm mixing in the angel [*mets l'ange*] next to the statue.*

– *Who are you thinking of?*

– *There is a Gandhi who walks near a square. I have always had a strange emotion with regard to statues. It is someone. The person himself, herself, the person is there, fortunately for him or for her, but sad, out in the cold. When I pass by.*

Montaigne, in the Latin Quarter.

– *They are there, the statues. And Balzac, do you greet him?*

– *The Balzac is hieratic, it is monumentalized.*

– *Are you thinking of your statue?*

– *Exactly. There is identification. When it's a matter of Gandhi, Montaigne, at the same moment I say to myself: 'at bottom it would reassure me to die knowing that there was a statue.' And then in a contrary movement, 'but that's worse than anything. They are there all alone out in the cold.'*

– *You want to be reassured anyway?*

– *At bottom.*

– *You can be reassured, you will have one*

– *But no I won't!*

– *What are you talking about?!*

– *But what are you talking about? Unless you take charge of it yourself right away. (he laughs)*

– *I'm not keen on it. I'd prefer to be on the balcony up there.*

– *I'm not asking you to do it, but all the same.*

Imagine that we were being overheard, here right now. Now here's a guy who is asking her to take charge very quickly after his death of having a statue erected to him.

— 'How not to obey you?' that's Derrida.

— Take time.

— I'm going to see to your statue, but not personally. I promise you that it will be done.

— It must be in the sun.

. . .

Good, let us leave ourselves a little time.

Notes

1. Jacques Derrida, 'Circumfession,' trans. Geoffrey Bennington, in Geoffrey Bennington and Jacques Derrida, *Jacques Derrida* (Chicago: University of Chicago Press, 1993), 26.
2. Jacques Derrida, *Geneses, Genealogies, Genres and Genius: The Secrets of the Archive*, trans. Beverley Bie Brahic (Edinburgh: Edinburgh University Press, 2006).
3. The French 'g' is pronounced like the English 'j,' whereas the French 'j' is pronounced like the English 'g.' (Tr.)
4. 'Circumfession,' 6–8.
5. 'Hearing' here translates *ouïe*. What cannot be rendered is the form of this word, in which can also be read and heard *oui*, yes, but with a feminine ending, as if to say: she who is yessed. Derrida also sounded this crossing between hearing and affirming in *Ulysses Gramophone:*

Hear Say Yes in Joyce, trans. Tina Kendall and Shari Benstock, in Derrida, *Acts of Literature*, ed. Derek Attridge (New York: Routledge, 1992). (Tr.)

6. Jacques Derrida, 'Psychoanalysis Searches the States of Its Soul,' trans. Peggy Kamuf, in Derrida, *Without Alibi*, ed. Peggy Kamuf (Stanford: Stanford University Press, 2002), 279.

7. Ibid., 240–1.

8. This is a reference to an essay-lecture by Derrida, 'Titre à préciser' ('Title to be specified'), the first section of which is titled 'Le titrier.' In the lecture, Derrida defies his audience to know whether, with this title, they are hearing two words, article plus obscure, perhaps invented noun, or else a four-word sentence: *Le titre y est*, the title is there. To *titrer*, titrate, is to ascertain the amount of a constituent in a chemical mixture; the French term also has the sense of assaying metals in alloys (cf. 'Titre à préciser' in Derrida, *Parages* [Paris: Galilée, 1986]). (Tr.)

9. Jacques Derrida, *H.C. for Life, That Is to Say . . .*, trans. Laurent Milesi and Stefan Herbrechter (Stanford: Stanford University Press, 2006), 7.

10. Ibid., 5.

11. Michel de Montaigne, 'On Friendship,' *Oeuvres complètes* (Paris: Gallimard, Bibliothèque de la Pléiade, 1967), 187.

12. *Geneses*, 18.

13. 'Va-t-il nous déchirer avec un coup d'aile ivre?': this is a first unmarked quotation from Mallarmé's sonnet, 'Le vierge, le vivace et le bel aujourd'hui.' In the following section, titled 'Aujourd'hui,' these allusions or quotations will proliferate. (Tr.)

14. 'Psychoanalysis Searches . . .,' 242–3.

15. Ibid., 257.

16. Ibid., 279–80.

17. *Tu*, the second-person familiar subject pronoun, has the same form as the past participle of *taire*, to silence, as in 'Il s'est tu,' he fell silent. (Tr.)

18. *Geneses, 30–1.*

19. *H.C. for Life*, 7.

20. Hélène Cixous and Jacques Derrida, *Voiles* (Paris: Galilée, 1998), 25; *Veils*, trans. Geoffrey Bennington (Stanford: Stanford University Press, 2001), 20; [henceforth, references will be given in the text to pages in both the original and the translation; citations from the translation will occasionally be modified to reflect as closely as possible Cixous's reading of Derrida's text. (Tr.)]

21. Don't lose the thread, that's the injunction that Penelope pretended to give herself, but also the feint or the fiction . . . 'Not even a question of pretending, as she did one day, to be weaving a shroud by saving the lost threads [*les fils perdus*: homonymically, the lost sons], thus preparing a winding sheet for Laertes, King of

Ithaca and father of Odysseus, for the very one that Athena rejuvenated by a miracle' (*Voiles*, 25; *Veils*, 22).

22. *H.C. for Life*, 2.
23. 'Psychoanalysis Searches . . .,' 256.
24. Ibid., 253.
25. Ibid., 256–7.
26. Ibid., 259.
27. The names. Names of Countries, Names of Cities. Good Airs [*Buenos Aires*], Saint Jacques, Saint Paul, bearers of signs, omens to which he lent an incredulous and worried ear. They exalt fears and desires by making these places more personal, thus more secret and more powerful.
28. 'Verdict' in Jacques Derrida: another subject for a thesis. *Verdict*, in French. Is there even *one* text that is not haunted by it?
29. 'Psychoanalysis Searches . . .,' 256.
30. Ibid., 256–7.
31. Reread here *Spirale*, no. 195, 'Fidélité à plus d'un,' March–April 2004. How past, terribly past, terribly present, how changed is this beautiful journal issue, concerned with the aporias of J.D. thinking. I want to pay tribute here to Ginette Michaud, a magnificent sleuth into the limbo of limbos, whose liminal explorations extend the critical continents to beyond the Thule islands, powerful and weak people like, let us say, the Inuits.

32. Jacques Derrida, *Resistances – of Psychoanalysis*, trans. Peggy Kamuf Pascale-Anne Brault, and Michael Naas (Stanford: Stanford University Press, 1998), 24–5.

33. Jacques Derrida, 'Fourmis,' in Hélène Cixous and Mireille Calle-Gruber, *Rootprints*, trans. Eric Prenowitz (London: Routledge, 1997), 119.

34. Ibid., p. 120.

35. *Resistances*, 27–8.

36. He almost always pities the child. Save – naturally, in the cases where it is the voices of women that he arranges to let protest apart from him in him, in those fictional dialogues expressing his compassion for women, his need for justice, his love for them, and thus the feminine part that he recognizes in himself.

37. *Resistances*, 12.

38. *Resistances*, 24.

39. 'Fourmis,' pp. 124–5.

40. The correct sentence would be: *Je ne sais pas ce que je peux faire*, I don't know what I can do. The mistake is to use the interrogative, *qu'est-ce que*, what is . . ., instead of the relative object pronoun, *ce que*. (Tr.)

Description of the Original Manuscript
of *Veils*

An autograph manuscript, written during a trip to South America in November 1995, and containing the first drafts of the text:

– A written sketch of the beginning, followed by a series of notes, titled 'Points de vue piqués sur l'autre voile,' five numbered sheets in the author's handwriting, 29 × 21 cm, in blue ink.

– Two states of a first draft titled 'Points de vue piqués sur l'autre voile, Buenos Aires, Le verdict'; one original in blue ink, the text crossed out with a line and the other photocopied, each consisting of ten numbered sheets in the author's hand, 29 × 21 cm, written on recto and bearing annotations or additions on verso.

– A new state, titled 'VER À SOIE,' bearing the subtitle 'Points de vue piqués sur l'autre voile,' nineteen attached tablet sheets, 29 × 20 cm, in black ink.

– A miscellaneous set of preparatory notes, drafts of sentences, indications of order, on diverse kinds of paper in different formats: four unnumbered sheets, two sheets on the back of memo paper from the Aspen Towers Hotel, one sheet on the back of a letter addressed to the author, 25 November 1995 from Buenos Aires, four unnumbered sheets folded in two, written in blue and blue-black ink, two sheets folded in four and showing the first indications of titles, one sheet from the note pad of the Grand Hôtel d'Europe in Saint Petersburg with a yellow annotated Post-it affixed, one sheet on the back of a bill dated 28 November 1995 from Edicial SA.

To these are joined two documents by Hélène Cixous, with the first states of 'Savoir':
    – A small cardboard-covered notebook (13 × 10cm), titled 'Dawn,' dated 19 January 1995.
    – Thirty tablet sheets (10.5 × 15.2cm).

All this is in a white cardboard file folder bearing the insignia of Harvard University, itself placed inside an orange cardboard folder with flap and elastic holder, 32 × 25cm, on which are numerous handwritten notes.